FIVE FINGE

A Play

by

PETER SHAFFER

SAMUEL   FRENCH

LONDON

NEW YORK TORONTO SYDNEY HOLLYWOOD

ISBN 0 573 01132 X

FIVE FINGER EXERCISE

Produced at The Comedy Theatre, London, on the 16th July 1958, with the following cast of characters:

(in the order of their appearance)

LOUISE HARRINGTON	*Adrianne Allen*
CLIVE HARRINGTON, her son	*Brian Bedford*
STANLEY HARRINGTON, her husband	*Roland Culver*
WALTER LANGER, a tutor	*Michael Bryant*
PAMELA HARRINGTON, the daughter	*Juliet Mills*

SYNOPSIS OF SCENES

The action of the Play passes in the Harringtons' week-end cottage in Suffolk

ACT I

SCENE 1 A Saturday morning in early September

SCENE 2 A Saturday night two months later

ACT II

SCENE 1 The following morning

SCENE 2 The same night

Time—the present

ACT I

SCENE I

SCENE—*The Harringtons' week-end cottage in Suffolk. A Saturday morning in early September.*

A multiple set enables us to see a fair amount of this little house: the living-room, the hall, the landing and the schoolroom where Pamela has her lessons. The living-room occupies all of the stage on the ground floor. It is well-furnished, and almost aggressively expresses Mrs Harrington's personality. We are let know by it that she is a "Person of Taste", but also that she does not often let well alone. There is more here of the town, and of the expensive town, than is really acceptable in the country: the furnishings are sufficiently modish and chic to make her husband feel, and look, perpetually out of place. There is a banquette or sofa R with a low coffee-table in front of it. A comfortable armchair C with a stool R of it, bridges the gap between the social centre of the room, and the dining section L, where there is a dining-table with three matching upright chairs above, below and L of it. There is an up-holstered bench R of the table. There are french windows L leading to an old garden. A glass-panelled door up LC leads to the kitchen. Up C is a sideboard. A contemporary lamp standard, with a basket shade is R of the sideboard and a tall pottery vase of flowers is in the corner R of the lamp. At night the room is lit by modern wall brackets, one R and similar brackets above and below the french windows. The light switches are by the door R and L of the kitchen door up LC. In the wall R, which comes down at right angles towards the audience before changing direc-tion to form a scrim behind the banquette, is the door into the hall. This can be seen, when lit, through the scrim wall. It is quite small and con-tains the usual paraphernalia of cottage halls: hats and coats on pegs, a small table with a telephone and a barometer. The front door is off R in the hall. A staircase in the hall leads on to the landing. This occupies a fairly small but important central area above the living-room where the back wall is "cut away". The door of Walter's bedroom opens on to the landing. This door is recessed and is not too prominent. From the landing a corridor leads off R to the bathroom and two bedrooms: Clive's and his parents'. At night the landing is lit by a wall bracket on a vertical pillar C, with the switch under it. R of the hall the staircase continues up to the schoolroom which is directly above the right side of the living-room. This is very much Pamela's room and is littered with her possessions, her books, old toys and clothes. Down C is a round table where her studies are done, with upright chairs above and below it. The entrance has a curtain but no door. The upstage wall contains the door

*to Pamela's bedroom. In the wall R there is a window, gaily framed in
frilly curtains. Under the window is a small set of bookshelves. A built-
in gas-fire is in the wall R. At night the room is lit by a wall-bracket R
with a switch above the entrance. The room is brightly coloured, and
reflects the liveliness of its chief occupant. The whole stage shows a
compact dwelling, disposed with feminine care.*

When the CURTAIN *rises, it is a bright morning. The table is set for
breakfast and* CLIVE HARRINGTON *is seated* L *of the table. He has
finished a plate of cereal and is engrossed in the morning paper. He is a
boy of nineteen, quick, nervous, taut and likeable. There is something
about him oddly and disturbingly young for his age, the nakedness of
someone in whom intellectual development has outstripped the emotional.*
LOUISE HARRINGTON, *his mother, enters from the kitchen, carrying a
plate of scrambled eggs. She is a smart woman in her forties, dressed
stylishly, even ostentatiously for a country week-end. Her whole manner
bespeaks a constant preoccupation with style, though without apparent
insincerity or affection. She is very good-looking, with attractive features,
which are reflected, though with greater instability, in Clive. She moves
to Clive, glancing out of the french windows as she passes.*

LOUISE. Your father's going back to nature. (*She takes Clive's
cereal plate and puts the plate of scrambled eggs in front of him*)
CLIVE. How far?
LOUISE (*putting the cereal plate on the sideboard*) Wait till you see.
(*She crosses to* L *of the table, pours coffee into Clive's cup then leans across
him and puts the coffee-pot and milk jug on the tray at the downstage end
of the table*) He's got one of his open-air fits. This morning we're
going shooting with that dreary stockbroker from the Gables—
what's his name . . . ? (*She picks up a napkin and lays it across Clive's
knees*)
CLIVE. Benton.
LOUISE. Yes. Well, to honour Mr Benton he's bought one of
those vulgar American hunting jackets made out of a car rug.
Can you imagine anything more ridiculous? (*She helps Clive to
butter*)
CLIVE (*eating his scrambled eggs*) He probably saw it in one of
those American mags that Chuck left here last week-end. Apart
from the jacket, how is he?
LOUISE. He's all right. Came down on the six-thirty. What
time did *you* get in?
CLIVE. Midnight.
LOUISE. Of course, he wanted to know where you were.
CLIVE. And did you tell him?
LOUISE. I didn't know. I suppose you were still in London.
CLIVE (*resentfully*) I was out. Just plain out.
LOUISE. Yes, dear. (*She crosses to the sideboard and picks up the
cereal plate*)
CLIVE. O-U-T.

LOUISE (*turning to Clive*) All right, dear. Could you manage another egg if I did one quickly? The pan's still hot.

CLIVE. No, thanks.

(LOUISE *exits to the kitchen.* CLIVE *hears* STANLEY *coming, quickly folds the newspaper and puts it on the upstage end of the table.*

STANLEY HARRINGTON *enters from the garden. He is a forceful man in middle age, well-built and self-possessed, though there is something deeply insecure about his assertiveness. He is wearing a brightly checked lumber jacket and is carrying a box of cartridges.* CLIVE'S *nervousness instinctively increases with Stanley's appearance*)

(*To Stanley*) Good morning.

STANLEY (*crossing above the table and putting the cartridges on the sideboard*) 'Morning. (*He turns towards the table*)

CLIVE. Very becoming.

STANLEY (*vaguely*) What?

CLIVE. I said, "very becoming".

STANLEY (*sitting at the upstage end of the table*) Oh.

(LOUISE *enters from the kitchen with a rack of toast which she puts on the table below Clive*)

(*To Louise*) Where's Pam?

LOUISE. Walter's taken her out for a walk before they start lessons. They've had their breakfast. I'll get yours. (*She moves behind Clive and kisses the top of his head*) Are you sure you don't want anything more, dear?

(STANLEY *reads the newspaper*)

CLIVE. Quite sure, thank you.

LOUISE (*fondly*) Well, you're having a good breakfast for a change. I shan't press you.

(LOUISE *exits to the kitchen. There is a slight pause*)

CLIVE (*nervously*) I think Pam likes to get the French over with early. Still, it's a bit desperate, starting the day with irregular verbs.

STANLEY (*brusquely*) You know who we are? We're millionaires.

CLIVE. What?

STANLEY. Now we've got a tutor we must be. We don't send our girl to anything so common as a school. You like the idea, I suppose?

CLIVE (*eager to agree*) As a matter of fact, I think it's ridiculous— I mean, well—unnecessary, really.

STANLEY. Your mother thinks different. Apparently the best people have tutors, and since we're going to be the best people whether we like it or not, we must have a tutor, too. Herr Walter

Langer, if you please. Ten quid a week and a whole term's fees to the school we didn't send her to. Did you know that?

CLIVE. No.

(LOUISE *enters from the kitchen with a plate of scrambled eggs and stands for a few moments up* L *of Stanley*)

STANLEY. Oh, yes. Still, I can afford it. What's money after all? We had a town place so we simply had to have a country place, with a fancy modern decorator to do it up for us. And now we've got a country place we've simply got to have a tutor.

LOUISE (*moving to* L *of Stanley*) Are you starting on that again? (*She puts the plate on the table in front of him*) Please remember it's Walter's first week-end down here and I want everyone to be very sweet to him. (*She moves behind Clive to the downstage end of the table*) So just keep your ideas to yourself, would you mind? We don't want to hear them. (*She sits at the downstage end of the table*)

STANLEY. We? Clive agrees with me.

LOUISE (*pouring coffee for Stanley*) Oh? Do you, Clive?

CLIVE (*quietly*) Isn't it a little early for this sort of conversation?

STANLEY. You just said you thought a tutor was ridiculous. (*He puts aside the paper and commences to eat his breakfast*)

CLIVE. Well, not that exactly. I mean . . . (*He lowers his eyes and proceeds to examine his breakfast with interest*)

STANLEY. What?

CLIVE. Well—not exactly.

LOUISE. Get on with your breakfast, dear.

(STANLEY *regards his son balefully. There is a slight pause during which* CLIVE *helps himself to toast and butter*)

STANLEY: You were in late last night. . . Why?

CLIVE (*avoiding his eye*) I—I got involved.

(LOUISE *signs to Clive to pass Stanley's coffee to him, then fills her own cup and helps herself to toast.* CLIVE *passes the cup of coffee to Stanley*)

STANLEY. Involved?

CLIVE. Well, I had some work to do in London.

STANLEY. Work?

CLIVE (*nervously*) Well, not exactly work—sort of criticism, really. I promised to review something. It's going to be printed . . .

STANLEY. In a paper?

CLIVE. Sort of paper.

STANLEY (*sarcastically*) Oh, *The Times,* I suppose?

CLIVE (*unhappily*) Well, it's more of a magazine, actually. It's not really—well, famous. You know . . .

STANLEY. What's it called?

CLIVE (*in a low voice*) *New Endeavour.*

STANLEY. New what?

CLIVE. Endeavour.

STANLEY. Well, what did they want to ask you for?

CLIVE. It was more me did the asking. You see, the usual man's ill, so I asked this friend of mine—who's a friend of the editor's if I could do it instead, and he said "yes". So I did. Anyway, it was two free seats.

STANLEY. What for?

CLIVE. A play. (*He smiles hopefully*)

STANLEY (*aloofly*) Was it any good?

CLIVE. Yes—it was splendid, as a matter of fact.

LOUISE. What was it?

CLIVE. *Elektra*.

STANLEY. What's that?

LOUISE (*with exaggerated surprise*) You can't mean it!

STANLEY. Mean what?

LOUISE. You just can't mean it. (*She stretches across the table and takes the newspaper*) Really, Stanley, there are times when I have to remind myself about you—actually remind myself.

STANLEY (*quietly*) Suppose you tell me, then. Educate me.

LOUISE (*loftily*) Clive dear, explain it to your father, will you? (*She opens the paper and prepares to read it*)

(CLIVE *continues eating*)

STANLEY (*to Clive*) Well, go on.

CLIVE (*in a low voice*) It's Greek.

STANLEY. Oh, one of those.

LOUISE (*putting her husband in his place; brightly*) Who was in it, dear? Laurence Olivier? I always think he's best for the Greek things, don't you? I'll never forget that wonderful night when they put out his eyes—you know the one; you and I went when your father was in Leeds that time. I could hear the scream for weeks and weeks afterwards, everywhere I went. (*She puts her napkin and the newspaper on the bench* R *of the table, rises and crosses to the coffee-table*) There was something so *farouche* about it. (*She takes a cigarette from the box on the coffee table, lights it with the table lighter, then takes a second cigarette from the box*) You know the word, dear: *farouche*? Like animals in the jungle.

STANLEY (*to Clive*) And that's meant to be cultured?

CLIVE. What?

STANLEY. People having their eyes put out.

CLIVE. I don't know what "cultured" means. I always thought it had something to do with those pearls they sell in Oxford Street.

LOUISE (*crossing and resuming her seat at the table*) Nonsense, you know very well what your father means. It's not people's eyes, Stanley: it's the *poetry*. Of course, I don't expect *you* to understand. (*She puts the second cigarette in Clive's mouth, picks up the news-paper and studies it*)

STANLEY (*to Clive*) And this is what you want to study at Cambridge, when you start there next month?

CLIVE. Well, more or less. (*He lights his cigarette with his pocket lighter*)

STANLEY. May I ask why?

CLIVE (*rising and crossing above the table to the sideboard*) Well, because—well, poetry's its own reward, actually—like virtue. All Art is, I should think. (*He picks up a copy of the "New Statesman" from the sideboard*)

STANLEY. And this is the most useful thing you can find to do with your time?

CLIVE (*moving down* RC) It's not a question of "useful".

STANLEY. Isn't it?

CLIVE (*sitting on the sofa*) Not really.

STANLEY (*staring gravely at him*) You don't seem to realize the world you're living in, my boy. When you finish at this university which your mother insists you're to go to, you'll have to earn your living. I won't always be here to pay for everything, you know.

CLIVE (*with a spurt of anger*) Look, I'm not exactly five years old.

(LOUISE *gestures to* CLIVE *not to argue, and he reads his paper*)

STANLEY (*extinguishing it*) Then it's time you acted your age. You're not a schoolboy any more. All this culture stuff's very fine for those who can afford it; for the nobs and snobs we're always hearing about from—(*he indicates Louise*) that end of the table, but it's not going to earn you the price of a sausage outside this front door. I mayn't be much in the way of education, but I know this: if you can't stand on your own two feet you don't amount to anything. And not one of that pansy set of spongers you're going round with will ever help you do that. And you know why? Because they've got no principles. No principles worth a damn.

CLIVE. You know nothing about my friends.

STANLEY. *I know.* I've seen them. Arty-tarty boys. They think it's clever going round Chelsea and places like that giggling and drinking and talking dirty, wearing Bohemian clothes. Tight trousers. Who gave them the right to look down on other people, that's what I want to know, just because they don't know about the—(*in an affected voice*) operah—and *ballay* and the *dramah*.

LOUISE (*still reading the paper*) And who gave you the right to talk about Bohemian clothes? What are you supposed to be, a lumberjack?

(STANLEY *rises, takes his pipe from his pocket, crosses, sits on the sofa at the left end and fills his pipe from the jar on the coffee-table*)

STANLEY (*ignoring Louise*) Who did you go with last night? (*He pauses*) Well? Who's this friend of the editor?

(Louise *stubs out her cigarette in the ashtray on the breakfast table, rises and puts Clive's and Stanley's cups and saucers on the tray*)

Clive (*subdued*) Chuck.

Stanley. Oh, yes. Your American pal. The one who stayed here last week-end—sings in cafés and wants to stay in school till he's thirty, living on grants.

(Louise *picks up the tray, crosses and puts it on the sideboard*)

Such a dignified way to go on.

Louise (*sharply*) I should have thought it was a sign of maturity to want to become more educated. (*She picks up a large wooden tray from the floor beside the sideboard, and moves to L of Stanley*) Unfortunately, my dear, we weren't all born orphans; we didn't all go to grammar schools, or work up a furniture factory on our own by sheer will-power. (*She crosses, puts the tray on the upstage end of the table and stacks the plates, etc., on to the tray*) We can never hope to live down these shortcomings, of course, but don't you think you might learn to tolerate them? We just didn't have the advantage of your healthy upbringing in the tough world outside. (*To Clive*) Jou-Jou, come and help me clear away, dear.

(Clive *rises, puts his paper on the sofa, crosses to L of the dining-table and clears everything remaining on to the tray, except the napkins, rings, ashtray and cloth*)

I'm going to get Walter to give me a music lesson later on.

Stanley (*rising and moving to the sideboard*) Music lesson! (*He takes the box of cartridges from the sideboard, transfers the cartridges from the box to a satchel from the armchair c, then puts the empty box on the sideboard*)

Louise. Certainly. And don't get yourself shot by mistake. Though there can't be many birds that colour.

Stanley (*irritably*) What time's lunch?

Louise. Oh, oneish. It depends. (*She pushes in the chair at the upstage end of the table, then stands up R of the table with her back to Stanley*) After my lesson I'm going to take Walter down to the bay. I'm going to show him some of the plants I've found. Did you know he was a botanist as well? And such charm! Well, of course, it's exactly what I've said all along. (*She picks up the loaded tray*) It takes a Continental to show us just how ignorant we really are. (*She moves to the kitchen door*) Jou-Jou. *La porte!*

(Clive *opens the kitchen door.*

Louise *exits to the kitchen.* Clive *returns to the table, collects the napkins and rings and puts them on the upstage end of the bench R of the table*)

Stanley. I'll see you later. That is, unless you want to come shooting with me? No, of course you wouldn't. Well, just see you get out in the air. I didn't take this cottage so you could lounge about indoors all day. You know, Clive, I just don't understand you at all. Not at all.

pe-set.

(STANLEY *picks up the satchel, goes into the hall, takes his hat from the pegs and puts it on, then takes his mackintosh from the pegs and exits by the front door, banging it behind him.*

LOUISE *enters from the kitchen and moves to R of the table*)

CLIVE (*sitting at the downstage end of the table; with dull rage*) Breakfast as usual.

LOUISE. It was just one of his moods.

CLIVE. Yes.

LOUISE (*sitting on the downstage end of the bench and taking Clive's hands in hers*) Oh, Jou-Jou, I want you to be very happy down here, darling. Really happy, not just pretending. After all, it's why I made daddy buy this place—to get away from the house and London and all the squabbling. To come into the country and relax in our own little retreat. So you've just got to be happy. You can't let me down. Can you?

CLIVE (*rising*) *Votre Majesté.* My Empress!

LOUISE (*permitting her hand to be kissed*) *Levez!*

CLIVE (*moving down L of the table*) The Empress Louise, ill-fated, tragic, dark-eyed queen from beyond the seas. What is your wish, madame? (*He makes a low bow to Louise*) I am yours to command. (*He moves above the table*)

LOUISE (*rising*) I've told you already, my little Cossack. *Sois content.* (*She takes the ashtray from the table and puts it on the bench R of the table*) Be happy.

(LOUSE *stands below the table and assisted by* CLIVE *removes and folds the cloth*)

CLIVE. *Bien.* On my honour as a guardsman, and on my beautiful hat of genuine black sheepskin, I promise to you six big laughs a day and twelve little giggles. (*He sits at the upstage end of the table*)

LOUISE (*moving to Clive with the cloth under her arm*) Darling. My darling Jou-Jou!

CLIVE. *Maman!*

(*They embrace very fondly*)

LOUISE. Now, that's a promise, you know. To be happy. Then I can be happy, too. Because I can tell when you're not, you know; and that makes me miserable also. So remember—no complexes. (*She moves and puts the cloth in the sideboard drawer*)

CLIVE. No complexes, *Majesté.*

LOUISE (*picking up the coffee tray*) Come on. I'll wash and you dry. (*She crosses and hands the tray to Clive*) They won't take five minutes.

CLIVE. It'll take at least twenty. (*He rises*) I can't think why you don't get a maid in.

LOUISE (*moving to the kitchen door*) Oh, Jou-Jou, not that again.

(CLIVE *moves to Louise*)

(*Warmly*) And, anyway, dear, this is meant to be a *retreat*. For just us. (*She takes a lump of sugar from the bowl and pops it into Clive's mouth*) Housework's all in the fun. Everyone does it these days.

(LOUISE *gives Clive a warm smile and exits to the kitchen.*
CLIVE *follows her off. The lights in the sitting-room dim and the lights in the hall, landing and schoolroom come up.*
PAMELA HARRINGTON *and* WALTER LANGER *enter the hall by the front door.* PAMELA *is a girl of fourteen, as volatile as her brother, and wholly without his melancholy or the seriousness that touches Walter.* WALTER *is a German youth, secret, warm, precise but not priggish and happily at ease with his young student. He is carrying a bunch of wild flowers*)

WALTER. Come on, we're ten minutes late already.

PAMELA (*running up the stairs*) If I get up there first—no French today.

(PAMELA *goes into the schoolroom and exits to her bedroom.* WALTER *follows her up the stairs into the schoolroom*)

WALTER. You're not going to get out of it that way. (*He calls into the bedroom*) Now we do the French. (*He moves to* R *of the schoolroom table and puts the flowers on it*)

(PAMELA *enters from the bedroom, having removed her coat*)

PAMELA (*moving to* L *of the table*) It's too cold to think in French, Walter.

WALTER. Very well. I'll light the fire. (*He takes a box of matches from the bookshelves, motions Pamela to sit* L *of the table, and lights the gas-fire*)

(PAMELA *sits resignedly* L *of the table*)

(*He replaces the matches, then sits* R *of the table*) And now—*parler* to talk. Future tense. Think hard.

(PAMELA *concentrates*)

PAMELA. *Je parlerai* . . . ?

WALTER. Good.

PAMELA. *Je parlerai, tu parleras, il parlera, nous—nous parlerons?*

(WALTER *nods*)

Vous parlerez, ils parleront.

WALTER. Good. That's the first time you have it right.

PAMELA. Oh, phooey to French. I hate it. Really.

WALTER. Why?

PAMELA. Because the French are a decadent nation. Personally I think we all ought to study Russian and American.

WALTER. But American is the same as English.

PAMELA. Of course it's not. When they say "dame" they mean young girl, and when we say "dame" we mean old girl. But when we call someone "old girl" we really mean what they call a dame. So you see.

WALTER. No.

PAMELA. Well, of course. I know all about American from Mary. You've still to meet her. She's my only friend here.

WALTER. Where does she live?

PAMELA. Over the stables in Craven Lane. You'll just fall when you see her.

WALTER. How? In love? (*He puts on his spectacles*)

PAMELA. Of course. Mummy says she's common, but that's just because she wears shocking pink socks and says, "Drop dead" all the time. I know her mother drinks and has lovers and things. But her husband's dead so you really can't blame her, can you? Just like Clive says: there-but-for-the-grace-of-God department.

WALTER. And she knows all about America because she says, "Drop dead"?

PAMELA (*loftily*) Of course not. How can you be so brutish? For one thing, she's got an American boy friend in the Air Force.

WALTER. How old is she?

PAMELA (*airily*) Sixteen. But that's all right; they like them young. I don't think they actually—well, you know . . . Sometimes, she gets decked up in her black jeans and goes off to some sexy club in Ipswich under a Polish restaurant. But her mother doesn't like her going round the streets looking like that, so she has to sneak off when no-one's looking.

WALTER. Like witches.

PAMELA. Witches?

WALTER. Going to their Sabbath.

PAMELA. What's that?

WALTER. When they used to worship the Devil. They used to sneak off just like that. It was the same thing like the Teddy Boys. You make yourself very excited, then people give you a bad name and start being afraid of you. That's when you really do start worshipping the Devil.

PAMELA. Oh, phooey!

WALTER (*more gravely*) Not phooey.

PAMELA. You talk as if you'd seen him.

WALTER. The Devil? I have.

PAMELA. Where?

WALTER. Where he lives.

PAMELA. Where's that?

WALTER. Where I was born.

PAMELA. And what was he doing?

WALTER. Sitting down.

PAMELA. Where?

WALTER. Behind people's eyes. (*He removes his spectacles. Seeing her confusion*) Well, isn't that a good place to sit?

PAMELA. Do you miss it?

WALTER. What?

PAMELA. Your home?

WALTER. It's not my home.

PAMELA. Still, there must be things you miss. Birthdays or Christmasses or something.

WALTER. Christmas, yes. Where I was born it was better. It's called Muhlbach. The stars are more clear there.

PAMELA. Just the stars?

WALTER (*with a small spurt of excitement*) No, ice, too. Ice grows all down the river, and at night you go skating all alone, all alone for miles in the black, and it's terribly cold and fast—and suddenly you see torches coming towards you, and voices come, and there's a crowd of happy people with nuts and fruit and hot rum, kissing you a good New Year.

PAMELA. Oh, wonderful!

WALTER (*putting on his spectacles; with reservation*) Yes, for that . . .

PAMELA. Let's go. Just for Christmas, you and me. You can teach me enough German in twelve weeks so I can understand everyone. Oh, I'm sorry. I forgot. You don't teach German.

WALTER. No.

PAMELA. Walter, I never asked before—but why not? I mean, you'd make more money doing that than anything else.

(WALTER *slowly shakes his head*)

You really are a very strange young man.

WALTER (*removing his spectacles*) Am I? (*He puts the spectacles into their case and pockets it*)

PAMELA (*kindly*) I suppose part of it's living in a foreign country all the time.

WALTER. It's not foreign. Not for always, anyway. I've been here five years, and soon now I get my citizenship.

PAMELA. Then you'll be English?

(WALTER *nods*)

Then you'll like Christmas here, too, because this'll be home and you'll spend it with us here in the country. Don't you have any family at all?

(WALTER *shakes his head*)

No-one?

WALTER. No.

PAMELA. But that's the wrong answer. When I say, "Have you got no family?" you must say: "Yes, of course I have a family, and a very fine one, too." Now, repeat after m.∵. "My family lives at twenty-two Elton Square, London, and 'The Retreat', Lower Orford, Suffolk."

WALTER. My family lives at twenty-two Elton Square, London, and "The Retreat", Lower Orford, Suffolk.

PAMELA. Good. Ten out of ten. (*She rises and moves to* R *of Walter*) Now, you look much happier. You should wear a high collar. And one of those floppy ties. Then you'd look like Metternich or someone. And wear your hair very sleek and romantic. (*She smoothes his hair*) Like this . . .

WALTER (*rising and dodging above the table*) Hey!

PAMELA (*moving to him*) No, it's terribly becoming. Count Walter Langer, Knight of the Holy Golden Soupladle. (*She ruffles his hair some more*)

WALTER. Pamela, no! (*He ducks away from the table, grabs the flowers and runs down the stairs on to the landing*)

(PAMELA *chases Walter. The lights in the schoolroom dim to a half. The lights in the hall and landing dim out. The lights in the sitting-room come up*)

Stop it! You're not to . . .

PAMELA. Pompous, pompous, pompous!

WALTER. Now, you stop it or I'll be very cross.

PAMELA. Augustus Pompous.

WALTER. And very sick.

PAMELA. Phooey!

WALTER. I will. You don't believe me?

(LOUISE *enters from the kitchen, carrying a music album*)

LOUISE (*as she enters*) Walter. (*She crosses to the hall door, opens it and calls*) Walter!

(LOUISE *leaves the door open, crosses and exits to the kitchen*)

WALTER (*calling*). Yes, Mrs Harrington? (*To Pamela*) There's your mother. I go now. What's that in French—"I go"?

PAMELA. *Je allez?*

WALTER. No, I've told you one million times. *Je vais.* Now, you go back and do some history.

PAMELA. Oh, all right. (*She goes up the schoolroom stairs and pauses at the top*) Hey.

WALTER. Yes?

PAMELA (*looking over the banisters*) See you anon, Mastodon.

(CLIVE *enters from the kitchen carrying a tray with clean cutlery, which he puts on the sideboard*)

WALTER. Quarter to four, Dinosaur. (*He goes down the stairs into the hall*)

(PAMELA *goes into the schoolroom, sits* R *of the table, applies herself to the history book and makes notes.* CLIVE *takes three knives and three forks from the tray and lays places at the table on the upstage end,* L *of it and the downstage end*)

(*He comes into the living-room*) Good morning.

CLIVE (*moving* L *of the table*) Hullo.

WALTER. Mrs Harrington was calling me.

CLIVE. She's in the music-room—through there.

WALTER. You have a music-room in this cottage? (*He closes the door*)

CLIVE. Only an outside one. When we took this place it used to be the scullery, but mother wasn't daunted by that, she picked up an upright for two pounds ten and knocked down a wall to get it in. It's lucky it's at the back because His Lordship doesn't care for music. (*He crosses to the sideboard and takes the two remaining knives and forks from the tray, then returns to* R *of the table*)

WALTER. Oh, I'm afraid I was playing the gramophone last night—I'm sorry.

CLIVE (*wryly*) He'll soon tell you if he minds. Tell me, how d'you like being tutor to our little hepcat?

WALTER (*moving to* R *of the armchair and putting the flowers on the sideboard*) Oh, she's delightful. When your mother first met me and invited me to live with you, I—I didn't know what I should find. My last job was—not so easy. Please let me help you.

CLIVE. Oh—thank you. (*He gives the knives and forks to Walter, then goes to the sideboard and takes five table mats from the drawer*) You lived with a family, too?

WALTER (*crossing to* R *of the table*) No. I had a flat in Paddington. (*He lays two places* R *of the table*) More of a basement, really. (*He picks up the napkins and rings from the bench, crosses below the table to* L *of it and puts the napkins at the various places*)

CLIVE (*crossing to* R *of the table*) I can imagine. (*He lays out the mats at the various places*)

WALTER. This is—my first family.

CLIVE. Yes?

WALTER. Yes.

CLIVE (*lightly*) Well, let me give you a warning. This isn't a family. It's a tribe of wild cannibals. (*He crosses to* R) Between us we eat everyone we can.

(WALTER *smiles*)

You think I'm joking?

WALTER. I think you are very lucky to have a family.

CLIVE. And I think you're lucky to be without one.

(CLIVE *sees a faint distress in* WALTER)

(*He sits on the sofa*) I'm sorry. (*He takes a cigarette from the box*) Actually, we're very choosy in our victims. We only eat other members of the family.

WALTER (*catching the mood*) Then I must watch out. (*He crosses above the table to Clive*) Your sister thinks I'm almost a member already.

CLIVE. Pam? (*He offers Walter a cigarette*)

(WALTER *shakes his head*)

You know, I don't like the way she's growing up at all. She wants to *include* people all the time: she doesn't appear to want to exclude or demolish anybody.

WALTER. Perhaps that's because she takes after her mother . . . (*Confused*) Excuse me.

CLIVE. That's quite all right. A girl who took after Stanley would be almost unthinkable.

(LOUISE *enters from the kitchen carrying the music-album*)

LOUISE (*crossing to Walter and putting the album into his hands*) Walter, my dear, I do hope I didn't disturb your lesson. I'm simply longing to hear you try my little piano.

WALTER. I should be delighted to, Mrs Harrington.

LOUISE. You have such beautiful hands. (*She sits in the armchair* C *and motions Walter to sit on the bench* R *of the table*) I remember once shaking hands with Paderewski.

(WALTER *sits on the bench, takes out his spectacles, puts them on and looks at the album*)

Of course it was many years ago, and I was only a girl, but I've never forgotten it. He had hands almost exactly like yours, my dear boy. Much older, of course—but the same bone formation, the same delicacy. That was my mother's album.

WALTER. It's charming.

LOUISE. What are you going to play for me? Something Viennese, of course.

WALTER. What would you like? Beethoven—Brahms?

LOUISE. Wonderful! And you can explain to me all about it.

(CLIVE *picks up his "New Statesman" and reads*)

I mean where it was written and who for. I always think it so much increases one's enjoyment if you know about things like that. Take the "Moonlight", for example. Now, what was the true story about that?

CLIVE. Well, it wasn't really moonlight at all, Mother. Moonlight was the name of the brothel where Beethoven actually was when he started writing it.

LOUISE (*shocked*) Jou-Jou!

CLIVE. He got one of the girls to crouch on all fours so he could use her back for a table. It's in one of the biographies, I forget which.

LOUISE (*to Walter*) He's being very naughty, isn't he? Really, Jou-Jou!

WALTER (*rising, moving to the sideboard and picking up the flowers*) I found these in the lane. They're quite rare—I thought you might be interested. (*He moves to L of Louise*)

LOUISE (*taking the flowers*) How very charming. I am very touched. Thank you, my dear. (*She pauses*) You know, I must give you a name. "Walter" is much too formal. Wait. Of course. (*She gets an idea from Walter's spectacles*) Clive's Jou-Jou, so you can be "Hibou". Perfect. Hibou, the owl. (*To Clive*) He looks rather like an owl, doesn't he?

CLIVE. Why not "Pou"? That's better still—"Louse".

LOUISE. Oh, he's impossible this morning. Your father's right, a walk in the fresh air would do you a lot of good.

(PAMELA *snaps her book shut and comes bounding out of the school-room and down the stairs*)

PAMELA (*running downstairs*) Mother! Mother!

LOUISE. Good Heavens, what a noise that girl makes. (*To Walter*) I'm afraid you're going to have to teach her some etiquette as well.

(PAMELA *comes bursting into the living-room.* WALTER *moves to the kitchen door and stands* R *of it, waiting for Louise. The lights in the schoolroom fade*)

PAMELA. Mother!

LOUISE (*rising*) Quietly, dear. Quietly.

PAMELA (*moving to* R *of Louise; breathlessly*) Sorry. (*She holds out a list of history questions*) Mother, will you test me on my history?

LOUISE (*moving to the kitchen door*) Ask Clive, will you, dear? I'm busy now. Walter's going to play for me.

(CLIVE, *on the sofa, slides on to his back with his head at the left end, and puts a cushion over his face*)

PAMELA. Are you, Walter? How marvellous.

LOUISE (*to Walter*) Come along, my dear. We haven't got too much time.

(LOUISE *exits to the kitchen.*
WALTER *follows her off.* PAMELA *studies Clive for a moment, then knocks on the cushion. She pauses, then moves behind the screen above the sofa, and knocks on it*)

PAMELA (*in a coy, exaggerated voice*) General—General Harrington. (*She puts her head round the screen*)

CLIVE (*in an "old soldier's" voice*) Eh? What's that?

(*The following dialogue is conducted in these voices.* CLIVE *sits up, rolls up his "New Statesman" and uses it as a telescope*)

PAMELA. May I come in?

CLIVE. Well, if it's not little Daphne. Spike me cannon! How very kind of you to call. Come in, me dear. Don't be afraid.

PAMELA (*mincing to the sofa*) Thank you. (*She sits* R *of Clive on the sofa*)

CLIVE (*putting his hand on her knee*) And how are you, eh? Eh?

PAMELA (*carefully removing Clive's hand*) Fine, thank you. (*She stretches out her left foot and points to it*) And how's the—(*she whispers*) you-know-what?

CLIVE (*in his normal voice*) Do I?

PAMELA (*in her normal voice*) Gout.

CLIVE. Ah. (*In the general's voice*) Oh, it comes and goes, y'know. Comes and goes.

PAMELA (*in Daphne's voice; gushing*) I think it's wonderful of you to take it so well. I'm sure I'd be complaining all the time. I'm a real silly-billy about pain.

CLIVE. Nonsense, me dear. Lord, though, how yer remind me of yer dear mother. (*He pulls a single hair from Pamela's head and holds it up to the light*)

(PAMELA *squeals*)

Hair just like hers. Yellow as a cornflower, I always used to say.

PAMELA (*in her normal voice*) There's something wrong about that.

CLIVE (*in his normal voice*) Is there? What?

PAMELA. Cornflowers are blue.

CLIVE. Well, your mother certainly didn't have blue hair.

PAMELA (*archly*) That's all you know. (*She hands the list of questions to Clive*) Anyway, you've got to test my history.

CLIVE. Your bow. (*He fixes the bow on her hair*)

(*The sound of piano music is heard off. It is the "Gavotte in D Minor; Bach: Sixth English Suite".* PAMELA *leans across Clive's knees, her right elbow on his left knee and her face cupped in her right hand*)

PAMELA (*listening*) He's the best, isn't he?

CLIVE. Just about.

PAMELA. Oh, you can tell. I knew just as soon as he came in the door.

(*They listen for a moment*)

CLIVE. How d'you get on together?

PAMELA (*rising and crossing to the armchair*) Oh, we simply adore each other.

CLIVE. Is he going to teach you anything?

PAMELA (*picking up Louise's handbag from the armchair*) Everything, my dear. (*She sits in the armchair, takes the mirror from the handbag and tidies her hair*) Just wait and see, I'll be the most erudine girl for my age in London.

CLIVE. Dite.

PAMELA. What?

CLIVE. Eru*dite*. (*He rises and crosses to the bench*) Well, come on, let's make a start. (*He studies the list earnestly for a moment*) Which was the most uncertain dynasty in Europe?

PAMELA (*replacing the mirror in the bag*) I haven't the faintest.

CLIVE (*as if reading*) The Perhapsburgs.

PAMELA. Who?

CLIVE. The Perhapsburgs.

PAMELA. Now, Clive, really . . .

CLIVE (*crossing to the screen; enthusiastically*) I don't know much about them yet, but I'm working on it. I'll have them fixed by the end of the week. So far there's just Thomas the Tentative—a successor of Doubting Thomas, of course—and—(*he sits on the coffee-table, facing Pamela*) Vladimir—the Vague.

PAMELA. That's marvellous! How about a woman?

CLIVE. By all means.

PAMELA. Dorothea.

CLIVE. Nice.

PAMELA. Dorothea the—the Downright.

CLIVE. But that's just the opposite. There's nothing "perhaps" about her.

(*The piano music ceases*)

PAMELA. Well, she could be the black sheep of the family.

CLIVE. We'll see. Now—(*he consults the list*) pay attention. Who was known as the Crying Cavalier?

PAMELA (*rising, putting the bag on the chair and crossing to Clive; protestingly*) No, Clive, seriously—I've really got to . . .

CLIVE. Answer me. Who?

PAMELA (*crossing to the bench*) I don't know.

CLIVE (*rising and crossing to Pamela*) Who was the Unknown Civilian?

PAMELA (*crossing below Clive to the sofa*) I don't know.

CLIVE (*following Pamela*) Who was the Curable Romantic?

PAMELA (*turning and gripping Clive by the throat*) I don't know. (*She forces Clive on to the sofa*) I don't know.

(CLIVE *struggles to his feet, gets* PAMELA *by the throat and forces her on to the sofa. Both are laughing*)

CLIVE. Really, you are the most impossibly ignorant child. (*He struggles happily with her*) Hepcat! Hepcat! Hepcat!

PAMELA (*pulling away from him*) Clive, tell me a story.

CLIVE (*sitting* R *of Pamela on the sofa*) Sweet or sour?

PAMELA. Sour.

CLIVE. All right. (*He pauses*) Once upon a time there was a little girl who lived all by herself in a prison.

PAMELA. Why? What had she done?

CLIVE. Nothing: that's just the point. They took away all her clothes and made her wear blankets instead.

(WALTER *enters from the kitchen; an obvious intruder*)

WALTER. Mrs Harrington was asking for her handbag.

PAMELA (*rising*) Here it is. (*She takes the handbag from the arm-chair and hands it to Walter*) Stay with us. (*She sits on the right arm of the armchair*) Clive's telling me a story.

WALTER. A story? About history?

PAMELA. About a prison.

CLIVE (*showing off to Walter*) Yes, it's going to be brilliant. All Gothic darkness and calamities. It's called the "Black Hole of East Suffolk". (*He rises and crosses to* LC; *mock grave*) Sit down and I'll unfold.

WALTER. No, not now. Your mother is waiting. Excuse me.

(WALTER *exits to the kitchen.* CLIVE *stares after Walter. His gaiety leaves him at once. There is a pause*)

PAMELA (*rising and moving above the table*) What's wrong?

CLIVE (*sitting on the bench*) Nothing.

(*There is a pause*)

(*In an everyday voice, almost brusque*) Come on, let's get on with your history.

CURTAIN

SCENE 2

SCENE—*The same. A Saturday night two months later.*

When the CURTAIN *rises, it is after dinner. The window curtains are closed and the lamps are on. There is a tray of coffee on the coffee-table.* LOUISE *is seated on the sofa at the left end with a cup of coffee in her hand. A copy of* "House and Garden" *is on the seat beside her.* STANLEY *is seated in the armchair which is now* RC. *He is smoking a cigar and reading a copy of* "Golf". *His coffee is on the stool* L *of his chair.* CLIVE *is standing at the sideboard, pouring a whisky for himself.*

LOUISE (*to Clive*) Don't you want any coffee?

CLIVE. No, thanks.

LOUISE (*putting her cup on the tray, rising and moving up* R) What are you drinking?

CLIVE (*crossing with his glass to the sofa, and sitting on it at the right end*) Whisky.

LOUISE (*moving to the sofa and sitting on it* L *of Clive*) I do think you might have caught an earlier train from Cambridge. I cooked a special dinner for you—all your favourite things—to welcome you home. (*She picks up her coffee*)

CLIVE. I'm sorry, Mother, but don't worry, I had a perfectly good sandwich from British Railways.

(*The sound is heard off of* PAMELA *practising the piano. It is a simple piece of Bach, being played over and over, with many wrong and repeated notes*)

LOUISE. Well, that's not enough for you.

(WALTER *enters from the kitchen, goes to the sideboard, picks up a gramophone record then moves towards the hall door*)

STANLEY (*referring to the piano practice*) How much longer now is that going on, may I ask?

LOUISE. For another half-hour, I hope. (*To Walter*) How's she getting on, dear?

WALTER. Oh, very well, Mrs Harrington. (*To Stanley*) It is only six weeks, you know, sir. (*He moves between Stanley and the screen*)

LOUISE. Yes, it's amazing, isn't it? Oh, Walter, would you mind taking Clive's suitcase upstairs as you go?

WALTER. Certainly, Mrs Harrington.

LOUISE. Thank you so much.

(WALTER *moves to* R *of the sideboard, picks up Clive's suitcase and scarf, goes into the hall, then on to the landing and exits* R)

(*To Clive*) I don't know why you can't put your own things away.

STANLEY (*to Clive*) And that's what you call great music?

(LOUISE *puts her cup on the tray*)

Is that right? Great music? (*He picks up his coffee, balances the saucer on the left arm of his chair and drinks his coffee*)

CLIVE (*with an attempt at humour*) Let's say it's a little distorted at the moment.

(LOUISE *rises, picks up the coffee tray and crosses to* L *of Stanley*)

STANLEY. Distorted? It's driving me mad.

CLIVE (*unhappily*) I suppose we can't expect her to be an expert in two months. Run-before-you-can-walk Department.

LOUISE (*picking up Stanley's saucer and jogging his arm with it*) Your father imagines that everything can be done without hard work.

(STANLEY *puts his cup on the saucer*)

Everything except making money out of the furniture business. (*She puts Stanley's cup and saucer on the tray, then moves above the arm-chair. To Stanley*) Really, you are absurd. How do you think Paderewski sounded when he was practising?

(WALTER *enters on the landing from* R *and exits to his own bed-room*)

What is that piece she's learning, dear? Mozart?

(CLIVE, *embarrassed, shrugs*)

Jou-Jou, I'm talking to you.
    CLIVE (*in a low voice*) Bach.
    LOUISE (*turning up* C; *rather annoyed*) You could play, too, if you wanted to. You've got the hands for it.

(LOUISE *exits to the kitchen. There is a pause*)

    STANLEY (*carefully*) Clive, do you remember coming to see me at the factory for your allowance the day you went up to Cambridge?
    CLIVE (*nervously*) Yes, I do.
    STANLEY. Did you have a talk to my manager while you were waiting?
    CLIVE. Did I, yes—I suppose I did. In a way . . .
    STANLEY. Yes. Is it true you told him you thought the furniture we make was—what was it—"shoddy and vulgar"? (*He pauses*) Well?"
    CLIVE. I think I said it—it lacked . . .
    STANLEY. What?
    CLIVE. Well, that it didn't use materials as well as it might. Wood, for example. (*He smiles hopefully*)
    STANLEY. And the design was shoddy and vulgar?
    CLIVE. Well—well, yes, I suppose I gave that impression. Not all of it, of course—just some things . . .
    STANLEY. What things?
    CLIVE (*plucking up a little courage*) Well, those terrible oak cupboards, for example. I think you call it the Jacobean line. And those three-piece suites in mauve moquette. Things like that . . .
    STANLEY (*impassive as ever*) Mr Clark said you called them "grotesque".

(CLIVE *lowers his eyes*)

Is that right—grotesque?
    CLIVE (*rising; mumbling*) I think they are, rather. (*He crosses with his glass to the bench* R *of the dining-table and sits, facing towards the windows. He puts his glass on the dining-table* L *of him*)
    STANLEY. And I suppose you think that's clever.

(LOUISE *enters from the kitchen*)

That's being educated, I suppose; to go up to my manager in my own factory and tell him you think the stuff I'm turning out is shoddy and vulgar. (*He pauses*) Is it?

LOUISE (*moving to Clive and picking up his glass which still has some whisky in it*) Just because *you've* got no taste, it doesn't mean we all have to follow suit. (*She registers disapproval of the drink, crosses and puts the glass on the sideboard, then moves to the sofa, picks up the copy of "House and Garden", sits on the sofa at the left end and opens it so that Stanley can see the title in time for his line*)

(STANLEY *gives* LOUISE *a look which silences her then turns again to* CLIVE *who continues to sit rigidly at the table*)

STANLEY. Now, you listen to me.

(CLIVE *picks up a book of essays from the table and reads*)

You get this through your head once and for all; I'm in business to make money. I give people what they want. I mean, ordinary people. Maybe they haven't got such wonderful taste as you and your mother: perhaps they don't read such good books—(*he peers at Louise's magazine*) what is it—(*He reads*) Houses and Gardens— but they know what they want.

(*A passage is repeated on the piano off several times, then there is an irritated bang on the keys and the noise stops*)

If they didn't want it, they wouldn't buy it, and I'd be out of business. Before you start sneering again, my boy, just remember one thing—you've always had enough to eat.

(*The explosive opening of the "Brahms Third Symphony, No. 3 in F Major, 1st Movement", is heard coming from a gramophone in Walter's room*)

(*He looks up. Dangerously*) One stops, the other starts. (*He rises and crosses to the hall door*) I'm going out.

LOUISE (*enjoying the music and beating time to it*) Where to—Mr Benton?

STANLEY. And if I am, at least I can get some peace there.

LOUISE (*still beating time*) Ssh!

STANLEY (*with a step towards Louise*) Don't you "ssh" me!

LOUISE (*putting down her magazine and turning to Stanley*) This is the first week-end we've all been here together since Clive went up to Cambridge. I think the least you can do is stay home, the first evening. (*She rises*)

(STANLEY *returns to the armchair and sits*)

Why must you be so disagreeable? (*She goes to the hall door, opens it and calls*) Walter. (*She goes on to the landing and calls again*) Walter.

(WALTER *enters the landing from his room, carrying a Brahms score*)

WALTER. Did you call, Mrs Harrington?

LOUISE. Do you think you could play your gramophone another time, dear? Mr Harrington has got a slight headache.

WALTER. Of course, Mrs Harrington.

(WALTER *exits to his room. The music stops, then* WALTER *re-enters*)

I'm so sorry. So very sorry.

LOUISE. That's quite all right, dear. Thank you very much. (*She moves towards the stairs, then turns back*) I hate to disturb your concentration.

WALTER. Oh.

LOUISE. Come down when you want to. (*She goes down the stairs to the hall*) I've got some delicious *petit fours*, and I'll make you some fresh coffee.

WALTER. Thank you, Mrs Harrington.

(WALTER *exits to his room and closes the door.* LOUISE *comes into the living-room and closes the door*)

LOUISE (*standing up* R *of Stanley*) Now, try and be a bit more pleasant, will you? (*She moves above the table, removing her rings from her fingers as she goes*) Jou-Jou, it's washing-up time, are you going to help me?

CLIVE. Can't we leave it for once?

LOUISE. It's all right. I can manage perfectly well without you.

(LOUISE *exits to the kitchen. There is a pause*)

CLIVE (*tentatively*) I'm sorry I said that about the furniture, Father. I suppose it was tactless of me.

(STANLEY *does not seem to hear. There is a pause*)

STANLEY. Never mind. How are you doing at Cambridge? What about the other boys, do you get on with them?

CLIVE (*turning and facing slightly towards Stanley*) It's not exactly like school, you know. You rather pick your own friends.

STANLEY. Yes, I suppose you do. Well, what do they do there? I mean, apart from lessons.

CLIVE. Anything you like. There are all sorts of clubs and societies.

STANLEY. Do you belong to any?

CLIVE. Well, I joined a Dramatic Society, as a matter of fact.

STANLEY. You mean for acting?

CLIVE. It's quite professional, you know. They have their own theatres and get reviews in *The Times*.

STANLEY. Don't any of them play any games?

CLIVE. Yes, but—well, the cricket and rugger are sort of professional standards. I thought of taking up fencing. It's not as odd as it sounds. It's meant to be very good for co-ordination . . .

STANLEY. What's that?

CLIVE. Muscles, I think.

STANLEY. Clive, as you know, your mother and I didn't see eye to eye over sending you to university. But that's past history, now. The point is, what use are you going to make of it?

CLIVE. That's rather as it turns out, I should have thought. I mean, you can't judge these things in advance, can you?

STANLEY. Ah, now, that's just what I mean. Clive, if you don't know where you're going you might as well pack up.

CLIVE. Why?

STANLEY. It's quite simple, I should have thought.

CLIVE. It isn't. It just isn't like that. I mean, if I knew where I was going, I wouldn't have to go there, would I? I'd be there already.

STANLEY. What kind of silly quibble is that?

CLIVE. It's not a quibble. Look, education—being educated— you just can't talk about it in that way. It's something quite different—like setting off on an expedition into the jungle. Gradually, most of the things you know disappear. The old birds fly out of the sky and new ones fly in you've never seen before— maybe with only one wing each. Yes, it's as new as that. Everything surprises you. Trees you expected to be just a few feet high grow right up over you, like the nave of Wells Cathedral . . . Anyway, if you had seen all this before, you wouldn't have to go looking. I think education is simply the process of being taken by surprise, don't you see?

STANLEY. Be that as it may . . .

CLIVE. You don't see.

STANLEY (*rising and moving* R *of his chair*) Clive, I'm not talking about education. (*He crosses above the armchair to Clive*) By all means, take advantage of your lessons. Look, my boy, let's not pretend. Everyone doesn't get to Cambridge: you know it and I know it. You're in a privileged position and you must make the most of it. What you do now, will influence the rest of your life. (*He sits above Clive on the bench*) You know that, don't you?

CLIVE. I suppose it will.

STANLEY. Take your friends, for example. What kind of friends do you have?

CLIVE. Do you want a list?

STANLEY. Now, don't start getting on any high-horse. I'm simply saying this: people still judge a man by the company he keeps. You go around with a lot of drifters and arty boys, and you'll be judged as one of them. I don't say you do, and you're old enough to decide for yourself, anyway. Right?

(CLIVE *nods*)

(*He takes the book from Clive, closes it and throws it on to the table*) Number twò is this. Now's the time for you to be making contacts with the right people, I mean people who will be valuable to you later on. I don't mean the smart people or the fancy la-de-da people your mother's always on about. I mean, the people who really matter. The people who have influence. Get in with them now, and you won't go far wrong. (*He rises and moves below the armchair*) I never had your advantages. (*He turns and faces Clive*) The contacts I made I had to work up myself. So I know what I'm talking about. Do you understand?

CLIVE. Yes.

STANLEY. You've got a good brain and I'll see to it you've got enough money. There's no harm in having a few quid in your pocket, you know.

(LOUISE *enters from the kitchen carrying a tray of clean forks and spoons*)

Don't ever be so stupid as to look down on money. It's the one thing that counts in the end.

LOUISE (*standing above the table*) Money! Is that all you ever think about?

STANLEY. You don't have any difficulty in spending it, I notice.

(LOUISE *gives Stanley a look, puts the tray on the sideboard and picks up the spoons*)

(*He crosses down* L *of the table. To Clive*) Now, let's see, how long have you been at Cambridge? Is this your half-term holiday?

LOUISE (*moving above the table*) Half-term! You talk about it as if it were a grammar school, instead of our leading university. Really, Stanley—(*she moves to the sideboard and puts the spoons in the drawer*) I don't know how one can even begin to talk to you.

STANLEY. (*furious; trying to control himself; to Clive*) Do you want to walk with me over to Benton's?

CLIVE. I—I've got some reading to do, actually.

(LOUISE *half-turns to watch Clive's reactions*)

STANLEY. We can stop in at the *Red Lion* for a quick one.

CLIVE (*after a pause; in a low voice*) No. I don't think so, really.

(STANLEY *looks up and sees Louise watching*)

STANLEY (*after a pause*) Very well.

CLIVE. It's important, or I would.

— (STANLEY *nods, crosses, goes into the hall, takes his coat and hat from the peg and exits by the front door.* LOUISE *looks after Stanley.*

CLIVE *turns slightly* L *and bangs his hand on the table*)

LOUISE (*moving to* R *of Clive*) Are you going to be intense?
CLIVE. No.

(LOUISE *sits above Clive on the bench. During the following speech,*
CLIVE *sits with his back to* LOUISE *who puts her hands on his shoulders,
smoothes and pats him and draws his head against hers*)

LOUISE. Oh, Jou-Jou! *Mon petit Cossack. Embrasse-moi.* (*She
pauses*) *Non?* (*She pauses*) It's your empress.
CLIVE (*rising*) Your Majesty. (*He crosses to the sideboard and pours
a whisky for himself*)
LOUISE (*rising and moving to* L *of Clive*) Every family has its
rows, you know. Come on, help me get the coffee—just the two
of us.
CLIVE (*moving down* R *with his drink*) In a moment, Mother.
LOUISE. All right, dear. But there's no need to take everything
as if it were one of your Greek tragedies.

(LOUISE *exits to the kitchen.* CLIVE *crosses to* R *of the bench.*
WALTER *enters the landing from his room, comes down the stairs
and enters the living-room. He carries a record catalogue*)

WALTER. May I come in? I'm so sorry about the noise—if I
had known I would not have played the machine.
CLIVE (*moving behind the armchair*) Yes, it's a pity. Music
always affects him that way. The better the music, the stronger
the headache. Do you want a drink?
WALTER. No, thank you.
CLIVE (*sitting in the armchair*) Was that the new record you were
playing?
WALTER (*sitting on the sofa; eagerly*) Yes. (*He puts the catalogue
on the seat beside him*) It's what's called "high fidelity". You know
—more bright and clear.
CLIVE. It sounds like the motto of a matrimonial agency.
"High Fidelity Guaranteed."
WALTER (*smiling*) It's nice to have you back, Clive. How are
you finding Cambridge?
CLIVE. It's all right, I suppose.
WALTER. Is that all? Just all right?
CLIVE (*suddenly alive*) No, it's wonderful. Like going to a new
country. Only I suppose one of the thrills of travel is hearing
people speak a foreign language. But the marvellous thing about
this is—well, hearing them speak my own for the first time.
WALTER. I know.
CLIVE. Pam speaks a few words of it, of course, but it isn't
quite enough. Where is she, by the way? Did she go for a walk?
WALTER. I think so, yes. (*He takes his spectacle-case from his
pocket*) It's a beautiful night.
CLIVE. Oh, yes. A night for walks. Pam tripping along so

gaily—father marching along so—rightly. And I should be by his side. Or, better still, a pace or two behind. "Clive, to heel, sir. Heel!" Let me introduce myself: "Spaniel Harrington". What's the matter?

WALTER. Nothing.

CLIVE (*mockingly*) Fathers should not be spoken to like that. Is that it?

WALTER. I think, if you forgive me . . .

CLIVE. Well?

WALTER. You have a duty to your father.

CLIVE. Duty? What a very German thing to say. Sorry, that's terrible, isn't it? Forgive me, I'm not quite sober.

WALTER. I did not mean duty like that. I meant that it seems to me—clever children have a duty—to protect their parents who are not so clever.

CLIVE. Protect?

(*The light in the kitchen is switched out*)

WALTER. I do not put it very well, perhaps.

CLIVE. Walter, I want to . . .

(LOUISE *enters from the kitchen. She carries a tray of coffee for one and a plate of petit fours*)

LOUISE (*switching off the wall-brackets* L) Hibou!

(WALTER *rises*)

I'm so sorry about the gramophone.

WALTER (*recovering*) Oh, it's me to be sorry. How is Mr Harrington?

LOUISE. It's nothing serious, my dear.

(CLIVE *fed up, rises, crosses and sits on the sofa at the right end*)

(*She crosses to Walter*) He's gone out to clear his head.

(WALTER *puts his spectacle-case on the down* R *corner of the coffee-table and takes the tray from Louise*)

(*She takes her rings from the tray, sits in the armchair and puts the rings on her fingers*) Well, now——

(WALTER *puts the tray on the coffee-table, pours himself some coffee, picks up the cup and saucer and sits* L *of Clive on the sofa*)

—we seem to have the house to ourselves. What are we going to do? I know! Walter shall recite some beautiful poetry for us, in German.

CLIVE. You don't understand German.

LOUISE. It's not the meaning, it's the sound that counts, dear. And I'm sure this boy will speak it adorably. Most people make it sound like a soda syphon, but when you speak it I'm sure I'll feel exactly what the poet wanted to say—even more than if I actually knew the language and how to cope with all those miller's daughters and woodcutters, and people. It's difficult to explain—but you know what I mean.

CLIVE (*rising*) I don't—I'm going out. (*He crosses below Louise and puts his glass on the sideboard*)

LOUISE. Where?

CLIVE. To the pub.

LOUISE. You can't be serious.

CLIVE (*moving up* L *of Louise*) Too vulgar?

LOUISE. Don't be silly, Clive. No, it's just so—uncivil, dear. There's plenty to drink in the house if you really need it, though I think you've had quite enough already.

CLIVE (*gravely*) You're right, I have. (*To Walter*) Excuse me. I'm sure you recite beautifully. (*He crosses above the table to the french windows*)

LOUISE (*rising and moving to* R *of the table; with a resurgence of desperation*) But your father asked you if you wanted to go to the pub and you said "no".

CLIVE. True.

(CLIVE *exits by the french windows.* WALTER *rises, puts his empty cup on the tray and stands stiffly. He is very uncomfortable*)

LOUISE (*crossing below the armchair to Walter*) Poor boy. I'm afraid he gets very upset down here. He's essentially a town person, really, like me. And I get it from my mother. Being French, of course. (*She takes a petit four and nibbles it*) Like all Parisians she detested the country. She used to say: "Fields are for cows, drawing-rooms are for ladies." Of course, it sounds better in French. What's the matter? Are you upset, too? Oh, Hibou . . .

WALTER. It is nothing.

LOUISE (*semi-humorously*) It is something. (*She sits on the right arm of the armchair, still nibbling*) Tell me—has Clive been teasing you? He can be very naughty.

WALTER. I think he is not very happy.

LOUISE. He gets that from me, too.

WALTER (*sitting on the sofa; impulsively*) Mrs Harrington—is there any help I can give? Anything at all?

LOUISE. I'm not a very happy person, either, you know. Well, you can see for yourself. (*Brightly*) Whatever you do, my dear boy, marry a girl who's your equal. If you can find one. I'm sure it'll be hard. (*Softly*) You see, when I married I was a very young girl. Believe it or not, I had hardly met anybody outside Bournemouth. My parents didn't consider it proper for me to run about on my own. And when I met Stanley they did everything in their power to arrange a marriage. You see, they weren't exactly very dependable people. My mother was an aristocratic little lady from France who'd never learnt to do a thing for herself all her life. My father was equally irresponsible: far too imaginative to make a good solicitor. (*She rises and looks in the coffee-pot to see if Walter has finished the coffee*) And when he actually inherited a little money, he lost it all in speculation. "Spec-u-lation." (*She picks up the coffee tray*) Do you understand, dear?

WALTER. Oh, yes.

LOUISE. Your vocabulary's really amazing. (*She moves and puts the tray on the sideboard. Over her shoulder*) Would you like a cigarette?

WALTER. Thank you, yes. (*He rises and takes a cigarette from the packet on the coffee-table*)

LOUISE (*moving to R of the armchair*) There. Where was I?

(WALTER *offers the packet to* LOUISE, *who refuses. He lights his cigarette with his own matches*)

Oh, yes, my parents. Well, they acted in my best interests: I'm sure that's how they saw it. They wanted me to have all the comforts they couldn't give me themselves. (*She moves below the armchair*) Father kept saying it was a—what was the word—a solid match. That's it. (*She sits in the armchair*) Stan the Solid: that's what I used to call him—as a joke, of course.

(WALTER *sits on the stool, facing Louise*)

And really, a bit of admiration, too, because my family was so *liquid*, if you like. Just the opposite, anyway. No-one ever worked consistently or made out budgets, so you see the man had his fascination. Naturally, father had reservations about the marriage. I mean, socially the thing was far from ideal, as I'm sure you realize. His people had always been professional men. Marrying me into the furniture business—(*with a faint smile*) well, it was rather like going into trade in the old days. Still, I was rather attracted to Stanley. I won't deny it. He had a sort of rugged charm. He was born with nothing, of course. His mother died in childbirth and his father was in the Merchant Navy. I gather he had a frightful time as a boy—but I will say this: it never showed in his manners. He was always terribly polite. Obviously, I was interested in all sorts of things like art and music and poetry which he'd never had time for. But when you're young, things like that don't seem to matter. It's only later— when the first excitement's gone—you start looking a little closer. Walter, these last few years have been intolerable. There are times when I listen to you playing, when I go almost mad with sheer pleasure, and yet year after year I've had to kill that side of myself, smother it, stamp it out.

WALTER. I'm so sorry.

LOUISE. Heaven knows, I've tried. I've tried to be interested in his bridge and his golf club, and in his terrible friends. I just can't do it. (*Intimately*) You know, don't you? You, of all people, must know.

(WALTER *looks down in embarrassment*)

I'm sorry. I didn't mean to talk like this. I'm embarrassing you.

WALTER. No.

LOUISE (*lightly*) I'm being vulgar, aren't I?

WALTER. You could never be.

LOUISE. Dear Hibou—you understand—you understand why I'm still here. The children. At least I could see that *they* weren't stifled, too. Do you condemn me?

WALTER. How could I condemn—in your house?

LOUISE (*wryly*) I think we can leave hospitality to one side.

WALTER (*pursuing his own thought*) In the house you have given me also to live in, so I can sit here by a fire and talk, as if always I had had the right.

LOUISE (*sympathetically*) Dear Walter.

WALTER. Where I worked before I taught the children for two or three hours, and then was paid by their mothers, and back always to my small room—(*with a faint smile*) with my cooking, which is not so good. You will never know how much I owe to you.

LOUISE. My dear boy. Tell me about your family. Your people in Germany.

(WALTER *stiffens perceptibly into withdrawal, rises and crosses above the armchair to* R *of the table*)

WALTER. There is nothing to tell.

LOUISE. There must be something.

WALTER. I was an orphan. (*He pauses, stands with his back to Louise and stubs out his cigarette in the ashtray on the table*) My parents died when I was too young to remember them. I was brought up by my uncle and his wife. (*He sits on the bench and faces Louise*)

LOUISE. Were they good to you?

WALTER (*noncommittal*) Very good, yes.

LOUISE. And—that's all you want to say?

WALTER. There is nothing else.

LOUISE. Don't think I'm being inquisitive. It's only that you've come to mean so much to us all in the last two months. You know that.

WALTER. I do not deserve it.

LOUISE (*warmly*) You deserve far more. Far, far more. I knew as soon as I saw you at that terrible cocktail party, standing all by yourself in the corner pretending to study the pictures. Do you remember? Before even I spoke to you I knew you were something quite exceptional. (*She rises and moves to* R *of Walter*) I remember thinking—"Such delicate hands—and that fair hair—it's the hair of a poet. And when he speaks, he'll have a soft voice that stammers a little from nervousness, and a lovely Viennese accent . . ."

WALTER (*rising and crossing to* R; *stiffly*) I am not Viennese, you know. I am German.

LOUISE (*moving above the armchair*) Well, it's not so very different.

WALTER (*doggedly*) I am German. This is not so poetic—even the name—I hate.

LOUISE (*a little intimidated by the darkness in him*) But, Hibou—(*she moves to him*) there's good and bad in all countries—surely?

WALTER (*turning to her; gently*) You are too good to understand what I mean. I know how they seem to you, the Germans: so kind and quaint. Like you yourself said: millers' daughters and woodcutters. But they can be monsters.

LOUISE (*prepared to mock him*) Really, now . . .

WALTER. Yes! (*He is plainly distressed*)

LOUISE (*sitting on the sofa and looking curiously at him*) You know, even in England, we're not all angels.

WALTER. Yes, angels to me. Because this to me is Paradise.

LOUISE. How charming you are.

WALTER (*with increasing heat*) No, I am sincere. Here in England most people *want* to do what's good. Where I was born this is not true. They want only power. They are a people that is enraged by equality. It needs always to be ashamed, to breathe in shame—like oxygen—to go on living. Because deeper than everything else they want to be hated. From this they can believe they are giants, even in chains. (*He recovers himself and sits* R *of Louise on the sofa*) I'm sorry. It's difficult to talk about.

LOUISE (*putting a hand on his*) Anything one feels deeply about is hard to speak of, my dear.

WALTER. One thing I know: I will never go back. Soon I'll be a British subject.

LOUISE. You really want to stay here.

WALTER. If you had seen what I have, you would know why I call it Paradise.

LOUISE. I can see for myself how you've suffered. It's in your face.

(WALTER *is plainly upset*)

Walter—(*very calmly*) you mustn't torment yourself like this. It's not good for you. You're among friends now. People who want to help you. People who love you. Doesn't that make a difference?

(WALTER *bends impulsively and kisses her hands*)

WALTER. You are so good! So good, good . . .

(LOUISE *suddenly takes Walter's head in her hands and holds it close to her*)

LOUISE (*tenderly*) Oh, my dear—you make me feel ashamed.

(CLIVE *unnoticed by the others, enters quietly from the kitchen, stands above the table and watches silently*)

It's been so long since anyone has talked like this to me.

(CLIVE *deliberately knocks a chair softly against the table*)

(*She rises and moves to* R *of the armchair*) Jou-Jou! (*She tries to recover her composure*) Have you had a nice walk? Did you see Pam?

(CLIVE *remains where he is, still staring at Louise*)

You know, it's absurdly late for her to be walking alone. Are you sure you didn't see her? She's probably gone over to that dreadful friend of hers—Mary whatever-her-name-is. She may have come in by the front door and I didn't hear.

(CLIVE *continues to stare*)

(*Her last remnants of poise desert her*) I'll just go up and see.

(LOUISE *goes into the hall, up the stairs to the landing and exits* R. WALTER *rises.* CLIVE *stands by the table. He is evidently fairly drunk, but alcohol does not impair his speech. Rather it gives it energy. He is more disturbed than he himself is aware*)

WALTER (*moving up* R *of the armchair and smoothing his hair*) Clive, what's the matter? Why are you looking at me like that?

CLIVE. Hair is being worn dishevelled this year. The Medusa style. What would have happened if Medusa had looked in a mirror? Are monsters immune against their own fatal charms?

(CLIVE *crosses to* WALTER, *puts an arm around his shoulders, leads him* R, *sits him on the sofa, then sits* L *of him*)

Observe, please, the subtle and dialectical nature of my mind. It's the French in me, you understand. An inheritance from my very French, very aristocratic ancestors. Perhaps you've been hearing about them. In actuality, I regret to say, they weren't as aristocratic as all that. My great-grandpa despite any impression to the contrary, did not actually grant humble petitions from his bedside—merely industrial patents from a run-down little office near the Louvre. The salary was so small that the family would have died of starvation if Hélène, my grandmother hadn't met an English solicitor on a cycling tour of the Loire, married him, and exchanged Brunoy for Bournemouth. Let us therefore not gasp too excitedly at the loftiness of mother's family tree. Unbeknownst to father it has, as you will see, roots of clay.

(WALTER *stares at* CLIVE *in silence, as he gets into his stride*)

Still, they *are* French roots. I even have them in me. For example —my mother's name for me—Jou-Jou. Toy. More accurately in this case, ornament. Being French, you know, mother imagines she's real ormulu in a sitting-room of plaster gilt. She suffers from what I might call a plaster-gilt complex, if you see what I mean. To her the whole world is irredeemably plebian—especially father. The rift you may detect between them is the difference between the *salon* and the saloon. At least, that's what she'd have you believe. I won't deny that she's only really at home in *salon*; but then where else can you be so continuously dishonest?

WALTER (*rising; stung into speech*) Please . . .

CLIVE. Yes? (*He rises*)

WALTER. I do not wish to hear this. (*He tries to pass Clive*) It's not right.

(CLIVE *puts a hand on* WALTER's *shoulder and pushes him back on to the sofa*)

CLIVE (*sitting L of Walter on the sofa*) Ah—you do not wish. The young *charming* tutor does not wish . . . So delicate, so old-world. A tutor and his employer by the fireside. Paris calling to Vienna! The waltz plays on the deserted boulevard; Europe crumbles. Oh, the charm of it. Do let's salvage what we can. If we can't have a château in Brittany, then we have a country place in Suffolk, which is almost as desolate but rather more convenient. If we can't install scholars in our library, because we haven't got a library, since nobody reads in our house, why then the least we can do is get in a dear gentle tutor for the girl, someone with tone, of course; nothing grubby from the Polytechnic. You see, we're specialists in delicacy.

WALTER. Why do you talk like this?

CLIVE. Because I'm not really so damn delicate, after all. Because actually, if you want to know, I'm getting less bloody delicate all the time.

WALTER (*rising and crossing to L of Clive*) I do not think I can listen to any more.

CLIVE. Where are you going?

WALTER (*gravely*) If you had come from Europe, if you had been taken in, as I was—alone—then perhaps . . .

CLIVE. Taken in! Taken in is right.

WALTER (*with a slight move*) Excuse me.

(CLIVE *rises, moves to* WALTER, *takes him by the shoulders and pushes him into the armchair*)

CLIVE. Or no—taken up! Like a fashion. Or an ornament; a piece of Dresden—a dear little Dresden owl.

(*There is a long pause as* CLIVE *leans over Walter, staring intensely into his face. Then* CLIVE *becomes aware of his position and moves his hands sharply away*)

And, believe me, like any other valuable possession, sooner or

later you will be used. (*He moves above the armchair*) I know this family, let me tell you. If you can't help one of us score a point over the others, you've no claim on our notice. Oh, my dear fellow . . .

(*The front door slams.*
PAMELA *enters by the front door and goes up to the landing. She wears her outdoor coat*)

LOUISE (*off* R; *calling*) Pam, is that you?

(LOUISE *enters on the landing from* R. CLIVE *stands in an attitude of listening, stock still.* WALTER *watches Clive uncertainly*)

PAMELA (*breathlessly*) Yes. It's all me. (*She goes up the schoolroom stairs*)

(CLIVE *moves to the screen and listens intently*)

LOUISE. It's rather late, dear. I wish you'd take your walks earlier.

(WALTER *rises, crosses below the table and stands up* L *of it*)

PAMELA (*removing her coat*) I'm sorry.
LOUISE. Where did you go?
PAMELA (*moving down the stairs to* R *of Louise on the landing*) Over to Mary's. You know, she is the absolute best: she tells the funniest stories in the world. D'you know what happened? Last week, Ted—that's her brother—took his daughter to the ballet. She's just eight, and it was a sort of extra birthday present. Well, she watched all these girls going up on their toes—(*she demonstrates*) and dancing about—and you know what she said at the end? "Daddy, why don't they just get *taller girls?*"

(PAMELA *laughs, realizes* LOUISE *is not reacting and stops short*)

Don't you think that's funny?
LOUISE. Yes, dear, very funny. (*She kisses Pamela*) Good night, dear.
PAMELA. Good night, Mother.

(LOUISE *exits on the landing to* R.
PAMELA *goes up the stairs to the schoolroom and exits to her bedroom, closing the door behind her*)

CLIVE (*calling*) Hepcat! (*To himself*) She's the only one who's free, with her private star of Grace. (*Louder*) It's a marvellous dispensation: to escape one's inheritance. (*He turns to Walter*) I don't mean you. Walter, you're one of the best people who ever came into our house. You think I don't know how lonely you were before you came here. I can smell your loneliness. You see, I've only one real talent—(*he moves to* R *of the armchair*) being

able to see what's true, and just what isn't. And that's an awful
thing to have. (*With sudden hunger*) Come away with me.

WALTER (*startled*) Come away? (*He moves below the table to* R
of it)

CLIVE. Look—in four weeks my term ends. Come away. Out of
this. We could go somewhere; to the West Country if you like.
Wells Cathedral is the most astonishing thing in England. It's
like walking down the throat of a whale: a skeleton whale, with
the vertebrae showing. No-one will be there at Christmas. Ched-
dar Gorge without a single charabanc. That's a bus, you know.

WALTER (*smiling*) Yes, I know.

CLIVE. Please say "yes". You'd love it.

WALTER (*with a shy smile*) I'm sorry. Christmas is a family
time. For so long I have missed it. This year I wish very much to
pass it here.

CLIVE (*insistently*) Well, afterwards. I could wait.

WALTER (*awkwardly; his whole stance awkward*) I'm afraid it's
not possible. My lessons, you see. I have been paid already to the
end of January.

CLIVE. So what? Everyone takes Christmas off.

WALTER. I do not think I can go away just now.

CLIVE. Because you've been paid?

WALTER. No.

CLIVE. Then why?

WALTER. I—I have an obligation.

CLIVE. To my mother?

WALTER. Yes. An obligation.

CLIVE. Is that what you call it—obligation? Well, doff my
plumed hat! Gallant Walter Langer—the Cavalier Tutor to his
Mistress. Or do I mean the Cavalier Teuton? Don't look so
startled. Proper cavaliers have only figurative mistresses. (*He
turns away, swept into frantic remorse. As before, he holds himself very
stiffly*) This is quite beyond anything, isn't it? (*With the quietness
of desperation*) If you came away with me, it would be for my sake
not yours. I need a friend so badly.

WALTER (*as stiff himself*) You are unhappy. I am sorry.

CLIVE (*the bitterness returning*) Is that all you can say—"I'm
sorry"? Such an awkward position I put you in, don't I? The
poor little immigrant, careful not to offend. So very sensitive.
(*With sudden fury*) When in hell are you going to stop trading on
your helplessness—offering yourself all day to be petted and
stroked? Yes! Just like I do . . . O.K., you're a pet. You've got
an irresistible accent. You make me sick!

WALTER. Excuse me. (*He crosses towards the hall door*)

(CLIVE *seeks clumsily to detain Walter*)

CLIVE. Walter, Walter, I didn't . . . Please . . .

(WALTER *goes into the hall and up on to the landing*)

(*He stands looking after Walter. To himself; intensely*) Please! (*He moves to the sofa and sits*)

    (PAMELA *enters from her bedroom, and comes down the schoolroom stairs, on her way to the bathroom. She wears pyjamas, dressing-gown and slippers.* WALTER *reaches the landing*)

PAMELA. Hullo? (*She recognizes Walter*) Oh, it's you.
WALTER (*turning to the door of his room*) Yes.
PAMELA. Is there anything wrong?
WALTER. No.
PAMELA. You look as if they were going to cut off your head in the morning.
WALTER (*turning to her; smiling with an effort*) Do I? You were walking?
PAMELA. Yes. Mary and I discovered a new place in the woods, with a huge stream you can dam up. I don't suppose it's anything compared with your river, the one you could skate on.
WALTER. You show it to me tomorrow?
PAMELA. Yes. (*She pulls aside her dressing-gown and points her toe*) Are you shocked because I'm in my this?
WALTER. Yes. Very.
PAMELA. Then you'd better leave, sir. I'm on my way to the bathroom. It is not my wish to cause you embarrassment.

    (WALTER *bows*)

(*She curtsies*) Good night.
WALTER. Good night.

    (PAMELA *exits on the landing to* R.
    WALTER *exits to his room.* CLIVE *rises, moves to the sideboard and pours a whisky for himself. He drinks.*
    STANLEY *enters by the front door, removes his hat and coat, hangs them on the peg in the hall, and comes into the living-room.* CLIVE *hastily moves up* L *of the armchair, leaving his glass on the sideboard*)

STANLEY (*seeing Clive move*) What are you doing?
CLIVE. Stealing your drink.
STANLEY. You don't have to steal from me, Clive. (*He goes to the sideboard and pours a whisky for himself*) You're old enough to take a drink if you want one.

    (CLIVE *crosses to the sofa, sits, takes a cigarette from the box on the coffee-table, lights it with the table-lighter and puts an ashtray on the seat beside him*)

Where's your mother?
CLIVE. I don't know—upstairs . . .

STANLEY. You ought to have come with me to Benton's. We went over to the club. Jolly nice crowd there. The sort of fellows *you* ought to be mixing with. There was a chap there in publishing. You'd have been interested. (*He pauses and crosses down* R) Clive, I've told you before, in this world you want to get in with the people who matter. But you've got to make an effort, my boy. Make yourself a bit popular. You see? And you're not going to do that sitting here drinking by yourself. Are you?

CLIVE (*in a low voice*) No, I suppose not.

STANLEY. What d'you want to do it for, anyway?

CLIVE (*shrugging*) I don't know.

STANLEY. Well, it's damn silly and it's not normal. If you want to drink—drink with others. (*He crosses and sits in the armchair*) Everyone likes a drink. You come over to the club with me, you'll soon find that out. I'll make you a member. You'll get in with them in a jiffy if you'll only try.

CLIVE (*stubbing out his cigarette in the ashtray beside him*) Yes. Well—(*he rises and moves to the hall door*) I think I'll go to bed, now.

STANLEY. Just a minute. What's that matter?

(CLIVE *stops and turns*)

Aren't they good enough for you? Is that it?

CLIVE (*gently*) No, of course it isn't.

STANLEY. Then what?

CLIVE (*moving to* R *of Stanley; gaining courage*) Well—all this stuff—right people, wrong people—people who matter. It's all so meaningless.

STANLEY. It's not a bit meaningless.

CLIVE. Well, all right, they matter. But what can I say to them if they don't matter to me? (*He crosses to the sofa and sits*) Look, you just can't talk about people in that way. It's unreal—idiotic. As far as I'm concerned, one of the few people who really matters to me in Cambridge is an Indian.

STANLEY. Well, there's nothing wrong in that. What's his father? A rajah or something?

CLIVE. His father runs a cake shop in Bombay.

STANLEY. Well, what sort of a boy is he? What's he like?

CLIVE. He's completely still. I don't mean he doesn't move. I mean that deep down inside him there's a sort of happy stillness that makes all our family rows and raised voices seem like a kind of—blasphemy almost. That's why he matters—because he loves living so much. Because he understands birds and makes shadow puppets out of cardboard, and loves Ella Fitzgerald and Vivaldi, and Lewis Carroll—(*he rises, moves and sits on the stool, facing down* L) and because he plays chess like a devil and makes the best prawn curry in the world. And this is him. Well, parts of him—bits of him.

STANLEY (*bewildered and impatient*) Well, of course I'm glad you've got some nice friends.

CLIVE. Don't. Don't do that.

STANLEY What?

CLIVE (*rising and crossing below Stanley to* L *of him*) Patronize. It's just too much.

STANLEY. I'm not patronizing you, Clive.

CLIVE. Oh, yes, you are. That's precisely what you're doing.

STANLEY. That's very unfair.

CLIVE (*working himself into a deep rage*) Precisely. Precisely! "I'm very glad you have some nice chums, Clive—I did, too, at your age." (*He moves to the sideboard and picks up his glass*) These aren't my little play-pals, Father. They're important people. Important to me.

STANLEY. Did I say they weren't?

CLIVE (*moving up* L *of the armchair; frantic*) Important! It's important they should be alive. Every person they meet should be altered by them——

(PAMELA *enters on the landing from* R, *goes up the stairs to the schoolroom and listens for a few moments*)

—or at least remember them with terrific—terrific excitement. That's an important person. Can't you understand?

(PAMELA *exits to her bedroom*)

STANLEY (*crushingly*) No, Clive. (*He rises, moves* R *of the armchair to the sideboard and puts down his glass*) I told you—I don't understand you at all.

(*There is a slight pause.* CLIVE *subsides. When he speaks again it is to renew the attack in a colder and more accusing voice*)

CLIVE. You're proud of it, too.

STANLEY (*moving up* R *of the armchair and facing Clive; getting angry*) What now?

CLIVE. That you don't understand me at all. Almost as if it defined you. "I'm the Man Who Doesn't Understand." (*Directly; his voice shaking with resentment*) Has it ever occurred to you that *I* don't understand *you?* No. Of course not. Because you're the one who does the understanding around here—or rather, fails to. (*Furiously*) What work did you ever put in to being able to understand anybody?

STANLEY. I think you'd better go to bed.

(*There is a pause as* CLIVE *puts his glass on the sideboard*)

CLIVE. I'll go to bed when I'm good and ready. (*He moves to* L *of Stanley*) D'you think it falls into your lap—some sort of a grace that enters you when you become a father?

STANLEY. You're drunk.

CLIVE. Yes, you think you can treat me like a child—but you don't even know the right way to treat a child. Because a child is private and important and *itself*. Not an extension of you. Any more than I am. (*He moves to the bench, sits on the downstage end, facing front and falls quiet, dead quiet, as if explaining something very difficult. His speech slows and his face betrays an almost obsessed sincerity*) I am myself. Myself. Myself. You think of me only as what I might become. What I might make of myself. But I am myself now—with every breath I take, every blink of the eyelash. The taste of a chestnut or a strawberry on my tongue is me. The smell of my skin is me, the trees and sofas that I see with my own eyes are me. You should want to become me and see them as I see them—as I should with you. But we can never exchange. Feelings don't unite us, don't you see? They keep us apart. And words don't help because they're unreal. We live away in our skins from minute to minute, feeling everything quite differently, and any one minute's just as true about us as any other. Yes, I'm drunk. You make me drunk.

STANLEY. I do?

CLIVE (*losing heart*) You and everything.

STANLEY. What are you talking about?

CLIVE. Nothing. It doesn't matter. Everything stays as it is.

STANLEY. Well . . .

CLIVE (*with a final spurt of energy*) I'm talking about *care*. Taking care. Care of people you want to know. Not just doing your best for them and hoping the best for them. I mean you've got to care for them as they are, from *blink* to *blink*. Don't you see? The—the renewing of your cells every day makes you a sacred object, or it should do in the eyes of people who care for you. It's far more important than whether you speculate in fish or furniture. Because what you do in the world, and so on, isn't important at all, not in the slightest, compared with what you look like and sound like and feel like as the minutes go by. That's why a question like—"What are you going to be?" is quite unreal. Do you see?

(*There is a long pause*)

STANLEY. Well, that's given me something to think about, old boy. It's getting late, now. Why don't we go on with it in the morning? What?

(CLIVE *is silent*)

Well, I'll say good night. (*He moves to the hall door and opens it*) I said "good night", Clive.

(CLIVE *still takes no notice.* STANLEY *shrugs and switches off the remaining lights, leaving the room lit by a glow from a spot in the foot-*

*lights, presumed to be a gas-fire. STANLEY moves into the hall, and
conscious of failure, goes slowly up on to the landing, where he pauses.
CLIVE rises, crosses to the coffee-table, takes Walter's spectacles from
the case and puts them on. He parodies Walter's half-bow; and then
peers at the room through the glasses— "seeing the world as Walter
sees it". Suddenly he takes them off, sinks on to the downstage end of
the coffee-table, and begins to cry terribly, almost silently. STANLEY
comes down from the landing, to the hall, goes into the living-room and
stands between the screen and the armchair)*

Clive, don't forget to turn out the fire. (*He moves above Clive*)
Clive. (*He kneels R of Clive and puts his hands on his shoulders*) What's
the matter, boy?

(*CLIVE shakes his head*)

You can tell me, can't you? (*He pauses*) Now, that's a silly attitude
to take, isn't it? I'm your father. That's what I'm here for.

(*CLIVE twists to face up stage from the thought of Stanley's touch*)

(*He rises*) I say, there's something really wrong, isn't there?
CLIVE (*whispering*) No. (*With the spectacles in his right hand, he
moves the hand behind his back to conceal them from Stanley, but it is
clear to the audience what he is holding*)
STANLEY. Did something happen while I was out?
CLIVE. No.
STANLEY. Well, what was it? Did mother say something? (*He
looks down, sees the spectacles and takes them from Clive*) Is it something
to do with Walter?

(*CLIVE rises, moves above the armchair and faces up stage*)

(*He moves above Clive and faces him*) That's it, Walter. Clive! What
happened with Walter?
CLIVE (*frightened*) I don't know. I don't know.
STANLEY (*seizing Clive; relentlessly*) Tell me what happened
with Walter?

(*They struggle together, then CLIVE disengages himself, pushes
Stanley to L and rushes to the hall door. STANLEY tosses the spectacles
on to the seat of the armchair. CLIVE pauses at the door, then suddenly
closes it and moves down L of the sofa*)

CLIVE (*after a pause*) It was mother.
STANLEY (*moving up R of the armchair*) What?
CLIVE. There on the sofa. I saw them. I came in and there
they were. (*He turns to face Stanley and stands close by the sofa*) The
light was turned down. They were kissing. *Kissing.* She was half
undressed. And he was kissing her, on the mouth. On the breasts.
Kissing . . .

(STANLEY *raises his arm as though to hit* CLIVE *who sinks on to the sofa, facing Stanley*)

(*Hard*) And before that, I think the light had been turned off.

(STANLEY *stares at Clive, stunned*)

(*He looks up at Stanley*) Department of Just Deserts?

CURTAIN

ACT II

Scene 1

SCENE—*The same. The following morning.*

When the CURTAIN *rises, it is a bright, cold day. The table is set for breakfast.* WALTER *is standing up* L *of the table, holding two plates with the remains of kippers.* PAMELA *is seated on the upstage end of the bench* L *of the table, reading "The Sunday Times", which is spread on the downstage end of the bench. She wears jodhpurs and shirt.* WALTER *crosses and puts the plates on the sideboard.*

PAMELA. Walter, what does "salacious" mean?

WALTER. What word?

PAMELA. "Salacious"—it's in this article.

WALTER (*moving to Pamela*) Show me. (*He picks up the paper*) Where are my glasses? (*He looks around, sees his glasses on the seat of the armchair, picks them up, puts them on and looks at the paper*) Ah, now—salacious. Yes, it means "wise". (*He returns the paper to Pamela, crosses above the table, sits* L *of it and drinks his coffee*)

PAMELA. Does it? I suppose I should have guessed. You ought to teach English.

WALTER. I wouldn't dare.

PAMELA. Oh, phooey! I'm sure you'd be miles better than the man at my last school. Anyway, he was a Dutchman. (*She looks at the paper*) Mother says this is the only Sunday paper she'll have in the house. I think it's mean of her. Everyone else has the popular ones with pictures of rapes . . .

(LOUISE *enters from the kitchen.* WALTER *immediately rises*)

LOUISE. Did you enjoy your kippers?

WALTER. Yes, they were splendid, thank you.

LOUISE. Do sit down, my dear.

(WALTER *resumes his seat*)

PAMELA. Mother, why can't we have Sunday papers with sexy pictures in?

LOUISE (*moving below Walter and looking in the coffee-pot*) Because they're vulgar, and give you a distorted view of life.

PAMELA. I don't mind.

LOUISE (*picking up the coffee-pot*) Well, I do. (*She moves above the table*) Where's Clive?

PAMELA. Not down yet.

LOUISE (*turning to Pamela*) Really, you children are the limit.

I just don't see why you can't have your breakfast together. It's late enough, heaven knows. Pamela, you'd better hurry up and finish dressing if you're going riding.

(LOUISE *exits to the kitchen.* PAMELA *puts the paper on the bench beside her*)

PAMELA. Have you ever gone riding?

WALTER. No.

PAMELA. It's the best, absolutely. What games did you play in Germany?

WALTER. I—I used to walk.

PAMELA. You mean on hiking parties, all dressed up in those leather shorts?

WALTER. No. By myself. I liked it better.

PAMELA (*impulsively*) Are you happy here? Are you really, really happy?

WALTER. Of course.

PAMELA. Who do you like best?

WALTER. You.

PAMELA. No, seriously.

WALTER. I like you all. You and your mother . . .

PAMELA. And Clive?

WALTER. Of course, and Clive. I like him very much. I'm only sorry he is so unhappy.

PAMELA. Is he very unhappy?

WALTER. I think so, yes.

PAMELA. That's because he was spoilt when he was young.

WALTER. Spoilt?

PAMELA. You know—spoil someone. Like damage.

WALTER. Oh, damage, yes.

PAMELA (*downright*) I'm sure he ought to get married. (*She drinks her coffee and puts the cup and saucer on the bench beside her*)

WALTER. Oh, he's so young.

PAMELA. For some people it's the best thing. You must help him find a girl.

WALTER. Has he not had friendships with girls before?

PAMELA (*in her "affected" voice*) Not even acquaintances, my dear. (*In her normal voice*) Except one: a girl called Peggy-Ann who worked in the tobacconist's when we were in the Isle of Wight. (*She spoons the sugar from the bottom of her cup*) She used to wear leopard-skin trousers and great sort of brass bells in her ears. Clive said they used to go down on the beach and neck, but I bet he was just bragging. So you see, you've got to help him. (*She rises, picks up her cup and saucer and puts them on the sideboard*) I'm sure you know hundreds of girls.

WALTER (*amused*) Oh, yes. What kind would you suggest?

PAMELA (*moving above the table*) Someone who'll pay him lots of attention. At home, everyone keeps on at him but no-one really takes any notice of him. (*Brightly*) Clive spends his whole time not being listened to.

WALTER. His mother listens, doesn't she?

PAMELA (*sitting at the upstage end of the table*) Not really listens, no. Well, of course, you can't expect her to. No mother ever really listens to her children. It's not done.

WALTER. You seem to know a lot about it.

PAMELA. Yes, I do. Poor Clive. You know, they really only use him to help them when they're rowing. (*Directly*) Can you understand why they row?

WALTER. I think everyone has quarrels.

PAMELA. Yes, but this is different. With mother and daddy the row is never really *about*—well, what they're quarrelling about. I mean—behind what they say you can feel—well, that mother did this in the past, and daddy did that. I don't mean anything *particular* . . . (*She stops, confused*) Oh, dear—I think marriage is a very difficult subject, don't you?

WALTER (*a little uncomfortable; humorously*) You don't take your exam in it till you're a little older.

PAMELA (*pursuing her own thought*) I mean, who begins things? Do you see?

WALTER. Please, Pamela . . .

PAMELA. I know mother's frightful to him about culture, and uses music and things to keep him out—which is terrible. But isn't that just because *he* made *her* keep out of things when they were first married? You know he wouldn't even let her go to concerts and theatres although she was dying to, and once he threw a picture she'd bought into the dustbin; one of those modern things—(*she gestures*) all squiggles and blobs.

(*The lights come up slowly on the stairs and hall*)

But then, mightn't *that* just have been because being brought up by himself he was afraid of making a fool of himself. Oh, poor daddy. Poor mother, too. (*Brightly*) You know, I shouldn't wonder if parents don't turn out to be my hobby when I grow up.

(STANLEY *enters on the landing from* R *and comes down to the hall. He looks tired and strained*)

WALTER (*warmly*) You have a wonderful mother, you know.

PAMELA. Yes, I suppose so.

WALTER. Only suppose?

PAMELA. People who make you feel stupid are always called wonderful.

(STANLEY *comes into the living-room*)

(*She rises and crosses to Stanley*) Good morning, Daddy. (*She kisses him then crosses above him to* R)

(STANLEY *stares at Walter with a curious unwilling stare*)

WALTER (*rising rather awkwardly*) Good morning, sir.
PAMELA (*to Stanley*) What's wrong? Aren't you feeling well?

(STANLEY *looks fixedly, almost unseeingly at Pamela, then sits slowly at the upstage end of the table.*
LOUISE *enters from the kitchen. She wears an apron*)

LOUISE (*as she enters*) Stanley? You might let me know when you come down. Walter dear, will you come and get Mr Harrington's cereal for me?
WALTER (*eager to help*) Of course, Mrs Harrington.

(LOUISE *exits to the kitchen*)

(*A little unnerved*) I hope your headache is better this morning, sir.

(STANLEY *nods, apparently unable to speak.*
WALTER *crosses, takes his cup and saucer from the sideboard and exits to the kitchen*)

PAMELA (*crossing to* R *of Stanley*) You aren't wearing your lovely coat.
STANLEY. No. I'm not going shooting today, darling, it's Sunday.
PAMELA. Well, come riding with me, then.
STANLEY (*wrapped in himself*) No—not today. I—just want to take things quiet.
PAMELA (*mischievously*) You're getting old.

(STANLEY *looks searchingly at Pamela*)

STANLEY. Why don't you ever learn to fix that bow. Come here.

(PAMELA *kneels* R *of* STANLEY *who fixes the ribbon*)

Has Clive come down, yet?
PAMELA (*rising*) No, the lazy pig. (*She sits on the left arm of the armchair*) You were talking to him late last night, weren't you? I could hear you from upstairs. Well, really, it seemed more like Clive was talking to you.

(STANLEY *stiffens but* PAMELA *does not notice.*
WALTER *enters from the kitchen, with a tea-towel over his arm, and carrying a plate of cereal which he puts on the table in front of Stanley*)

WALTER (*impersonating a waiter, for Pamela's benefit*) Mrs Harrington asks would you prefer eggs or kippers?
STANLEY (*quietly*) Nothing.
PAMELA. Daddy, you must have something.

STANLEY (*rising*) Don't fuss, Pam. Nothing. (*To Walter. Curtly*) Nothing. (*He sits on the bench with his back to the table*)
WALTER (*with a half bow*) Very good, sir.

(WALTER, *deflated, exits to the kitchen. There is a pause*)

PAMELA (*sliding into the armchair*) He'd make a wonderful waiter, wouldn't he? (*She pauses*) How did you like Clive talking to you man to man? (*Brightly*) He must have been drunk.
STANLEY. Why do you say that?
PAMELA. Because if he wasn't, he never would have. Not properly, anyway. He'd be too nervous.

(STANLEY *looks sharply at Pamela*)

That's because you like him to answer questions all the time, and he hates to.
STANLEY. Why?
PAMELA. I don't know. I suppose he's just not the answering type. D'you know he even has a dream about you?
STANLEY. Clive does?
PAMELA. Yes. He gets it quite often, so he must think an awful lot about you. You ought to be flattered, though it's not exactly what I'd call a flattering dream. (*She recounts it carefully, with increasing drama*) Apparently he's always in bed lying down under thick blankets; near him is a window and he can see into a big garden all covered in snow. It's freezing so hard he can hear twigs snapping on the trees. Then suddenly you appear, coming slowly over the snow towards him—(*she rises and crosses step by step to Stanley in time with her words*) crunch—crunch—crunch. (*She sits above Stanley on the bench*) You disappear inside the house and he can hear you coming upstairs—crunch—crunch—and along the passage to his bedroom. Then the door slowly opens and you come in, and cross the room to see if he's asleep. So while you stand there he pretends to be asleep as asleep can be, except that sometimes he starts shivering, which spoils the effect. Then you start taking off the blankets one by one. Clive says there must be about ten blankets on the bed, and with each one you take off he gets colder and colder. Usually he wakes up with all his bed-clothes on the floor. Isn't that the silliest dream you ever heard? I told him the next time he heard you coming upstairs he was to wait till you came up to the bed, then sit bolt upright and shout, "Go to hell!"

(STANLEY *has listened to this impassively, but with the greatest attention. He still sits involved in his own silent conflict.*
LOUISE *enters from the kitchen with the refilled coffee-pot*)

LOUISE (*moving down L of the table*) Pamela! Are you still here? (*She puts the coffee-pot on the tray*) You're going to be very late for your ride.

(PAMELA *rises and moves towards the hall door*)

And I've told you before, unpunctuality is just bad breeding.

(WALTER *enters from the kitchen, crosses to the coffee-table* R *and collects his spectacle-case*)

PAMELA (*to Walter*) I've decided you'd make the most wonderful waiter.

LOUISE (*shocked*) Pamela! What a thing to say.

PAMELA. Well, he would. Can't you just see him bowing to old ladies with Pekineses. (*She mimics*) "This way, please, madame, your table on the terrace is reserved for you as usual." (*She extends her hand as if for a tip*)

LOUISE. Stop it, Pamela! That's very rude. Can you think of nothing better for Walter to be? I only hope when you grow up you'll have a tiny part of his education. (*To Walter*) And his lovely manners. (*She sits at the downstage end of the table and pours a cup of coffee for Stanley*) Now, hurry up and get dressed.

(*The lights come up slowly on the landing and schoolroom.*
WALTER *goes into the hall and up the stairs into the schoolroom and selects a book from the shelves*)

Your sandwiches are all ready.

PAMELA (*moving to* R *of Stanley*) Daddy, can I borrow your red jacket? Please say "yes".

STANLEY (*quietly*) Of course—it'll be a bit big, though, won't it?

PAMELA. Nonsense—I shall wear it as a cape. (*She crosses to the hall door*) Of course I won't look half so good in it as you do.

STANLEY. Enjoy the ride.

PAMELA (*intimately*) You bet.

LOUISE. And tell Clive from me, if he's not down right away, he won't get any breakfast.

(PAMELA *goes into the hall and collects her riding cap and crop*)

Stanley, what are you sitting there for? I hear you didn't want any cooked breakfast. And you haven't even touched your cereal. That's absurd. You must have something to eat.

(STANLEY *stares at Louise*)

What is the matter?

(PAMELA *goes on the landing and moves to the door of Walter's room*)

PAMELA (*calling*) Walter.

LOUISE (*to Stanley*) Did you have too much to drink last night or something?

(STANLEY *rises and crosses above the table to the french windows*)

Stanley . . .

(STANLEY *exits abruptly by the french windows.* LOUISE *stares at him in astonishment, then rises, collects the newspaper from the bench, resumes her seat and reads the paper.* WALTER *comes down from the schoolroom with his book*)

PAMELA (*turning*) Walter.
WALTER (R *of Pamela on the landing*) Hello.
PAMELA. I wasn't really rude just now, was I?
WALTER. No, of course not. As a matter of fact, I was a waiter once, for a short time in Berlin. But they threw me out.
PAMELA. Why?
WALTER. No dignity. That's what they said. (*He crosses to the door of his room*)
PAMELA. How ridiculous! You're the most dignified man I ever met.

(PAMELA *exits on the landing to* R *and is heard knocking on Clive's door and calling*)

(*Off; calling*) Clive! Wake up, wake up, whoever you are!

(PAMELA *re-enters on the landing, carrying Stanley's hunting coat*)

(*She continues to call*) Into your slippers, go down for your kippers. (*She goes up the stairs to the schoolroom*) Wake up, wake up. (*She puts her cap and crop on the table and the coat on the chair* R *of the table*)

(CLIVE *enters on the landing from* R, *carrying his jacket over his arm, and goes up the stairs to the schoolroom. He is tousled and has a slight hangover*)

CLIVE (*bowing in Oriental fashion to Pamela*) Good morning.
PAMELA (*bowing; in the act at once*) Salaams. A thousand welcomes, O handsome slave boy, mine eyes rejoice in the sight of you. (*She moves to Clive, seizes him and swings him round*) Dance for me, my little pomegranate. Madden me with desire.
CLIVE. Drop dead! (*He goes down the schoolroom stairs, sees Walter, pauses and stares at him for a moment*) Good morning.
WALTER. Good morning. Excuse me. I 'think I work a little.

(WALTER *exits to his room.* CLIVE *stares after him for a moment, then puts on his jacket.* PAMELA *picks up her cap and crop and the jacket and moves to the top of the schoolroom stairs*)

CLIVE (*to Pamela*) Where is everybody?
PAMELA. Downstairs. You'd better go down.

(CLIVE *groans and moves to the hall stairs*)

You look a bit green. Do you want a fizzy?

CLIVE. No, thanks.
PAMELA. Well, salaams.
CLIVE. Salaams.

(PAMELA *exits to her bedroom.* CLIVE *goes slowly downstairs and into the living-room. He is clearly reluctant to go. He gets a cigarette from the box on the coffee-table, and lights it*)

LOUISE. You slept late. Perhaps you had a little too much to drink last night, too.

(CLIVE *crosses in silence to the table*)

There's kippers or eggs.
CLIVE. No, thank you. Is there any coffee?
LOUISE. Now, what is this? First your father and now you. (*She pours a cup of coffee for Clive*)
CLIVE. Where is he?
LOUISE. Outside.
CLIVE (*crossing above the table to the french windows; perplexed*) Where?
LOUISE. In the garden. (*She pauses*) Well—isn't he? (*She reads her paper*)
CLIVE (*looking off* L) Yes. He's sitting down under the apple tree.
LOUISE. *Sitting?* In this weather! Without an overcoat? He'll catch his death. Tell him to come in at once.
CLIVE (*crossing above the table to the bench*) Perhaps he prefers it outside. (*He sits on the downstage end of the bench with his back to the table*)
LOUISE. Don't be ridiculous, Clive. The man must be mad, sitting out there on a freezing morning like this. What on earth he thinks he's doing, I can't imagine—carrying on like that.
CLIVE (*sharply*) Leave him alone!
LOUISE (*lowering the paper; amazed*) Are you talking to me?
CLIVE (*almost surprised at himself; firmly*) Leave him alone.
LOUISE. Are you sure you're feeling all right?
CLIVE. I—I'm sorry.
LOUISE. So you should be. That was very, very ill-bred.
CLIVE (*whispering*) Not really done?
LOUISE. Clive, I don't understand you this morning. I really don't.

(CLIVE *smiles wryly to himself*)

CLIVE (*with a French accent*) Votre Majesté should not worry 'erself about eet. (*He takes his cup of coffee from the table*) It makes, as the Eeenglish say, no nevaire mind. (*He toasts Louise with his cup*) Your Majesty. (*He replaces the cup on the table and extends his hand in salutation*)

(LOUISE, *made uncertain by the mockery in Clive's manner, warily allows her own hand to be taken and kissed. At the same moment the second movement of Brahms' Third Symphony Number 3 in F Major is heard on the gramophone from Walter's room. For a moment* LOUISE *and* CLIVE *listen to the music. Their eyes meet.* LOUISE *drops the newspaper on to the floor beside her and holds out her arms.* CLIVE *kneels to her and she embraces him. He returns the embrace fondly, almost desperately*)

LOUISE. Jou-Jou . . .
CLIVE. *Maman!*
LOUISE. *Mon petit—mon petit* . . . (*She holds him tenderly, in the position of subservience he took up before his Empress, only now very close to her. From his posture she can fondle his head*) Darling. D'you think I'm so stupid I don't know what's wrong? D'you think I can't see for myself? (*She holds his face in her hands*) We're a little bit jealous, aren't we?

(CLIVE *moves sharply*)

(*She continues to hold him*) As if you didn't always come first. You know that. Don't you?

(CLIVE *nods, stiff now with reluctance*)

(*She puts her arms around him*) Then it's so ridiculous, isn't it, to be jealous. And of who? A poor lonely boy with no people of his own to care for him, all by himself in a foreign country. Really, Jou-Jou, you ought to be ashamed. (*She kisses his forehead*) Let's say no more about it. I want you always to be happy—remember? Very, very happy.

(CLIVE *nods*)

There. (*She releases him*) Now, come and help me get your breakfast. You could eat an egg, couldn't you?
CLIVE (*rising and sitting on the bench; in a low voice*) I suppose so.
LOUISE (*rising and moving to the kitchen door*) Good. You finish your coffee while I get started. (*She looks at him tenderly, moves to him and kisses him on the forehead*) Silly—silly boy.

(LOUISE *exits to the kitchen*)

CLIVE (*with a sort of bitter disgust; to himself*) On waves of sympathy. On waves . . .

(CLIVE *rises, takes his cup and saucer to the sideboard, glances out of the french windows and exits hurriedly to the kitchen.*
STANLEY *enters from the garden. He crosses slowly above the table to the screen* R, *pauses a moment, witlessly, his eye blank, his gestures aimless, then goes into the hall, closes the living-room door, takes his hat and mackintosh from the hall pegs and exits by the front door,*

banging it after him. During this CLIVE *watches Stanley through the kitchen door curtain and disappears when Stanley exits.*

PAMELA *enters the schoolroom from her bedroom, carrying her cap and crop, and the hunting coat. She puts the cap on the back of her head, picks up her sandwich tin from the table and goes down the schoolroom stairs, "conducting" the music with her crop and trailing the coat. She trips on the coat, misses her footing and falls in an undignified heap on the landing, dropping everything. Her cap falls off)*

PAMELA. Damn! Damn! Damn!

(*The music ceases abruptly.*
WALTER *rushes out of his room, startled by the crash*)

WALTER. What's the matter, Pamela? I help you . . . (*He picks Pamela up in his arms*) Are you hurt?
PAMELA (*indignant at being found like this*) No, I just tripped down those stairs.
WALTER. Are you all right?
PAMELA. Yes, of course I'm all right. Walter—put me down.

(LOUISE *enters from the kitchen, carrying an egg whisk.*
CLIVE *follows her on.* LOUISE *crosses towards the hall door, pauses a moment and hands the whisk to Clive*)

LOUISE. Here, take this. (*She goes into the hall and runs up the stairs*) Pamela! Is that you? What's the matter?

(CLIVE *follows to the hall door, listens a moment, then closes the door, crosses and exits to the kitchen.* PAMELA, *realizing she is being held, begins kicking her legs.* WALTER *stands Pamela on her feet*)

PAMELA. I'm all right—don't fuss, Mother. Anyone would think I was dying. (*She feels her head*) Ow!
WALTER (*picking up Pamela's property*) See? You bumped your head.
PAMELA (*witheringly*) When you fall down, you must bump something. It's usual.
WALTER. I look.
PAMELA. No.
LOUISE (*moving between Pamela and Walter*) My darling, are you all right? What happened, Walter?
WALTER (*concerned*) She fell. I think you should look on her head.
LOUISE (*taking Pamela's property from Walter*) Thank you, Walter. I'll see to it. (*To Pamela*) Now, go along upstairs.
PAMELA (*going up the stairs into the schoolroom*) Fuss, fuss, fuss.

(WALTER *gives his half bow and exits to his room.* LOUISE *follows Pamela into the schoolroom*)

LOUISE. Now—sit down. (*She puts the crop, cap and tin on the table and the coat on the chair* R *of the table*)

(PAMELA *sits* L *of the table*)

(*She examines Pamela's head*) Let me see. Does it hurt?

PAMELA. No, it doesn't.

LOUISE. You say that as if you wanted it to. What on earth were you doing?

PAMELA (*exasperated*) Nothing. I just tripped on that stupid coat. And that idiot Walter has to come in and pick me up as if I was a chandelier or something. Holding me that way.

LOUISE (*carefully*) What way, darling?

PAMELA. Well, trying to carry me, as if I was a baby.

LOUISE (*crossing above Pamela to* L *of her*) But he was only trying to help you—wasn't he?

PAMELA (*angrily*) I think he's just plain soppy.

LOUISE. Because he was worried about you?

PAMELA. Oh, Mother, for heaven's sake! You don't understand anything. It's just so *undignified*, can't you see? It shows no *respect* for you. I mean, if you're two years old it's all right to pick you off floors that way, and even then it's an invasion of your privacy. If children of two could speak, you know what they'd say: "Why can't you keep your filthy hands to yourself?"

(LOUISE *crosses behind Pamela, picks up the cap, crop and tin from the table and Pamela's jersey from the chair* R)

LOUISE. I think you'd better be off on your ride before you get into any more trouble.

(PAMELA *rises and moves towards the schoolroom stairs*)

(*She picks up the coat and hands it to Pamela*) Here—take this.

PAMELA (*going down the stairs to the landing*) Oh, it's one of those mornings.

(*The lights in the schoolroom fade to a half*)

I bet you anything the horse breaks its leg.

(LOUISE *follows Pamela on to the landing. As they reach the landing the music from Walter's room recommences*)

D'you think Walter heard what I was saying just now?

LOUISE (R *of Pamela*) Well, you weren't exactly whispering, were you? Now, come along.

(LOUISE *and* PAMELA *go down the stairs and into the living-room. While they are on their way and the stage is empty, the gramophone record sticks. The passage is repeated four times, then the needle is moved on*)

PAMELA (*moving down* LC) I think I'm the most impossible person I know.

(LOUISE *leaves the hall door open and crosses to* R *of Pamela*)

But then I suppose wonderful people always make you feel like that. Sort of ashamed all the time.

LOUISE. He makes you feel ashamed?

PAMELA (*taking her cap from Louise*) Not exactly ashamed, but, well, like in those advertisements for washing powder. I always feel like the grubby shirt next to the dazzling white one. (*She puts on her cap*) He's so fresh. Fresh and beautiful. (*Brightly*) Don't you think he's beautiful?

LOUISE (*handing Pamela the crop and sandwich tin; confused*) I hadn't thought.

PAMELA. It's just what he is. (*She picks up the newspaper from the floor and puts it on the bench*) He should wear a frock-coat and have consumption.

LOUISE. What nonsense.

PAMELA. Why? There *are* people like that.

LOUISE (*with sudden irritation*) Well, Walter certainly isn't one of them. He's obviously quite a happy, normal young man. There's simply no reason for you to weave any romantic ideas about him being tragic or different in any way.

PAMELA (*moving down* L; *grandly*) I'm afraid it's obvious you don't know him very well.

(LOUISE *is unamused. Instead, she is making an effort at self-control*)

LOUISE. If you're going, you'd better go. (*She holds out the jersey*) And put on your jersey.

PAMELA (*moving to* L *of Louise*) Oh, phooey.

LOUISE. Darling, it's cold out.

PAMELA. It isn't, really.

LOUISE. Pam, it's very cold. Now, do be sensible.

PAMELA. Mother, I can't put on any more—I'd just die.

LOUISE (*pushing the jersey into Pamela's hand; snapping*) Do as I say. Put on your jersey.

(LOUISE *turns abruptly, goes into the hall, then up the stairs to the schoolroom. She closes the living-room door behind her.* PAMELA *looks after her in surprise*)

PAMELA (*puzzled*) 'Bye.

CLIVE (*off in the kitchen*) Pam, is that you?

PAMELA (*crossing below the table to the french windows*) I'm just off.

(*The music ceases.* LOUISE, *in the schoolroom, takes a pile of clean linen from the chair* R, *sits* L *of the table and sorts the linen.*)

CLIVE *enters from the kitchen carrying a plate of scrambled eggs and a fork)*

CLIVE *(putting the plate on the upstage end of the table)* What were you doing? Playing at being the Walls of Jericho?

PAMELA. Oh, shut up!

CLIVE. Well, have a good time. *(He gets the newspaper from the bench, sits at the upstage end of the table and eats his breakfast)*

PAMELA *(turning to Clive)* You should come with me.

CLIVE. I know. It does you good to get into the air.

PAMELA *(in a wildly affected, cheerful voice)* Well then, bye-bye, darling. You're sure there's nothing I can get you from the village? A barrel of beer? Harris tweed?

CLIVE *(matching her accent)* No, thanks, old girl. Just bring back the usual papers, will you? The *Hunting Gazette* and the *Shooting Gazette.*

PAMELA. Righty-ho! *(She moves to the french windows and opens them)*

CLIVE. And the *Fishing Gazette*—and some wax for the old moustache.

PAMELA. Certainly, dear.

CLIVE. I say, Pamela—you are a brick!

PAMELA *(blowing him loud mock kisses)* Cheeribye, darling.

*(*PAMELA *shimmies out by the french windows.* CLIVE *eats his breakfast and reads the paper.*

WALTER *enters from his room carrying the Brahms' score. He glances up at the schoolroom, then comes down the stairs and into the living-room.*

LOUISE *rises and exits to Pamela's bedroom)*

CLIVE *(to Walter)* Hullo.

WALTER. Hullo.

CLIVE. Do you know that a judge trying a copyright case in this country once asked learned counsel: "What exactly *are* Brahms?"

*(*WALTER *smiles in appreciation, closes the door and moves a little* c)

CLIVE. What's the matter with your record?

WALTER. It's not the record—the needle keeps jumping. It's the table, I'm afraid, which is not quite level.

CLIVE *(putting down the paper)* Oh, really? It must be one of father's. Well, how are you? Clearly unwell, I should say. Only the sick and corrupt would spend a bright Sunday morning listening to music. You must know that in all decent English homes this time is reserved for sport. Staying indoors is the absolute proof of decadence.

WALTER *(moving* c) Yes. This is familiar to me. Where I was born—to sit reading was an offence, too.

CLIVE. You had to be out playing games?

WALTER (*crossing to* L *of Clive*) Games. But in small uniforms.

CLIVE (*scenting difficulty*) I suppose every kid wants to be a soldier.

WALTER. Oh, yes. (*He pauses*) But in England they are not told it is a good thing to be.

CLIVE. Did your uncle believe it was?

(WALTER *does not reply*)

(*Cheerfully*) Well, parents and guardians are desperately unreliable. It's what I've been telling you for weeks.

WALTER (*smiling*) Maybe we expect too much of them. After all, they are only us, a little older.

CLIVE. Older and more depended on.

WALTER. Exactly.

CLIVE. So not a bit like us. Absolute Power Department.

WALTER (*mischievously*) Do you think *you're* going to make a very good father?

CLIVE. I don't see why not. I was a complete success as a baby. I was so demanding, I gave my parents the idea they were indispensable.

WALTER (*amused*) You must have been a terrible boy. (*He sits* L *of the table*)

CLIVE. Oh, desperately average, I think. Stamp collection and all.

WALTER. I wish I had known you then.

CLIVE. What on earth for?

WALTER. It would have been nice when I was a child.

CLIVE (*speculatively*) Sometimes you make me wonder if you ever were.

(WALTER *lowers his eyes*)

(*He goes on with a rush*) But you're such an *excluded* person. It's the thing about you.

WALTER (*softly*) Not now.

CLIVE. Then what now?

WALTER (*not looking at him*) Now—I am at home.

CLIVE. And what's that?

WALTER (*still not looking at him; embarrassed*) Home, 1 think, is where people——

CLIVE. Yes?

WALTER. —people who really know you will want to find you.

CLIVE. And you want to be found here. With us?

(WALTER *does not reply*)

You poor goop.

(*There is an embarrassed pause*)

(*Briskly*) Have you always wanted to be a teacher?

WALTER. Oh, yes. Since I was fifteen.

CLIVE. I think that's splendid. I wish *I* had something positive I wanted to be.

WALTER. Haven't you?

CLIVE (*gaily*) No. I only know what I *don't* want to be. But there really isn't anything I could give a life to. The trouble is if you don't spend your life, other people spend it for you. As I see it, unless I suddenly hear a call from above, I'm going to wind up unemployable.

WALTER (*rising, crossing and putting his music score on the sideboard*) I don't think so. Life attracts you too much. (*He moves to the armchair*)

(CLIVE *shrugs*)

CLIVE. I always seem to be talking about things that don't matter.

WALTER. Of course they matter.

CLIVE. Oh, in a way. Talking's always so beside the point. So easy—so . . . I don't know. The real thing's always somewhere else.

(*The two contemplate each other. There is a short pause*)

WALTER. Clive, I'm sorry I ran out on you last night.

(CLIVE *stiffens and pushes his plate away so as to leave a clear space on the table in front of him*)

CLIVE. Let's forget it.

WALTER. It was kind of you to suggest a holiday together.

(CLIVE *looks at him woodenly*)

(*He sits on the left arm of the armchair*) I know you're not happy here—I would be honoured if you could talk to me. If there are things you want to say—like last night I felt there were things.

CLIVE (*darker*) I think we'll forget it. (*He pauses. In difficulty*) Walter, don't take me wrong—but are you sure you did the best thing when you left Germany?

WALTER (*surprised*) You think I should go back?

CLIVE (*not looking at him*) I think you ought to try.

WALTER (*in amazement*) You talk as if you wanted me to go away.

CLIVE (*very quiet*) Yes.

WALTER. Why?

(CLIVE *does not reply*)

Last night you did not want it.

CLIVE (*with sudden desperate anger*) Last night . . . I want it now. I want you to go. (*He modifies his tone with an effort*) For your sake. Only for your sake, believe me. You've got a crush on our family that's almost obscene. Can't you see how lucky you are to be on your own? Just because you never had a family you think they're the most wonderful things in the world.

WALTER. Clive . . .

CLIVE. Why have you got to depend all the time? It's so damned weak.

WALTER. You know nothing.

CLIVE. I can see.

WALTER. What? My parents? My father—can you see him, in his Nazi uniform?

CLIVE. But—you told me they died.

WALTER. No. They are alive. Back in Muhlbach. Alive. There was no uncle. (*He rises and crosses above the table to the window*)

CLIVE. Your father was a Nazi?

WALTER (*looking out of the window*) Oh, yes. He was a great man in the town. People were afraid of him, and so was I. When war broke out, he went off to fight and we did not see him for almost six years. When he came back, he was still a Nazi. Now, everyone else was saying, "We never liked them. We never supported them." But not him. "I've always supported them," he said. "Hitler was the best man our country has seen since Bismarck. Even now we are defeated, we are the bravest country in Europe. And one day we will win, because we have to win." (*He crosses above the table and sits on the downstage end of the bench*) Every night he used to make me recite the old slogans against Jews and Catholics and the Liberals. When I forgot, he would hit me—so many mistakes, so many hits.

CLIVE. But your mother?

WALTER. She worshipped him. Even after we found out.

CLIVE (*rising and crossing to* C) What?

WALTER. That during the war—he worked at Auschwitz concentration camp. One of the most efficient officers. (*He pauses*) Once he told me how many . . . (*He stops in distress. His voice dead with loathing*) I could have killed him. Killed him till he was dead. And she worshipped him—my mother. She used to smile at him, stare at him—as if he owned her. And when he hit me, she would just—just look away, you know, as if—what he was doing was difficult, yes—but unavoidable, like training a puppy. That was my mother.

CLIVE (*after a pause*) And so you left?

(WALTER *nods*)

I'm sorry.

WALTER (*recovering*) So you see, I do know what it is to have a family. And what I look for. (*In a strange tone*) A house where now and then good spirits can sit on the roof.

CLIVE. And you think you've found it here? Do you?

(WALTER *does not answer*)

You're fooling yourself every minute.

WALTER (*gravely*) Don't you think I should find that out for myself?

CLIVE. Oh, for God's sake! If that horrible story was meant to change my mind, it didn't.

WALTER. I did not tell it for that.

CLIVE. Then go. Just get the hell away from here.

WALTER (*rising*) Clive—my friend . . .

CLIVE. For my sake—*I* want it.

WALTER. But why?

CLIVE. Because—(*he moves towards the hall door*) I can't bear to watch.

WALTER. I don't understand you.

CLIVE. Well, then, just *because*. (*He turns towards Walter*)

(LOUISE *enters from Pamela's bedroom and comes down on to the landing*)

Because. Because . . .

LOUISE (*calling*) Walter.

(WALTER *looks enquiringly at Clive, unwilling to court interruption*)

CLIVE (*hard*) Go on. Answer her. It's your duty, isn't it?

WALTER (*in a low appealing voice*) Clive . . .

CLIVE (*turning ferociously on him*) Answer her.

(WALTER *stands irresolute.*

CLIVE *crosses above the table and exits abruptly by the french windows, slamming the windows after him.* WALTER *follows Clive and stands at the windows looking after him.* LOUISE *comes into the hall*)

LOUISE (*calling*) Walter.

WALTER (*looking after Clive; faintly*) I'm in here, Mrs Harrington.

(LOUISE *comes into the living-room and closes the door behind her. The lights in the schoolroom and landing dim*)

LOUISE. Ah, there you are, my dear boy. All alone? (*She sits in the armchair*) Come and talk to me, it's not good for you to be on your own too much.

WALTER. I was not alone. Clive was here. He's just gone out.

LOUISE. Out? Where?

WALTER. I don't know. (*He crosses above the table and sits on the bench*) Mrs Harrington, I'm a little worried for him.

LOUISE (*smiling*) Poor Hibou, you worry about everybody,

don't you? But you mustn't about Clive, really. It's just a tiny case of old-fashioned jealousy, that's all. Well, it's only to be expected, isn't it? He and I have always been so wonderfully close.

WALTER (*courteously*) Of course.

LOUISE. It's nothing serious. One day he'll understand about women. At the moment, of course, he thinks there must be room in my heart for only one boy. So silly. (*Warmly*) I don't believe you can ration love, do you?

WALTER (*admiringly*) With someone like you it is not possible.

LOUISE. Nor with you, my dear. You know, last night held the most beautiful moments I've known for many years. I felt—well, that you and I could have a really warm friendship. Even with the difference—I mean in—in our ages.

WALTER. Between friends there are no ages, I think.

LOUISE (*tenderly*) I like to think that, too.

WALTER. Oh, it's true. Like in a family—you never think how old people are, because you keep growing together.

LOUISE. Yes.

(WALTER *rises, crosses to* R *and stands with his back to Louise*)

What's the matter, Little Owl, are you embarrassed?

(WALTER *shakes his head*)

That's the last thing you must ever be with me.

(WALTER *smiles*)

What are you thinking? Tell me.

WALTER. Some things grow more when they are not talked about.

LOUISE. Try, anyway. I want you to.

WALTER (*turning and moving to* R *of Louise*) It is only that you have made me wonder . . .

LOUISE (*prompting eagerly*) Tell me.

WALTER (*lowering his voice*) Mrs Harrington, forgive me for asking this, but do you think it's possible for someone to find a new mother?

(LOUISE *sits very still and stares at Walter*)

(*He kneels beside Louise and puts his hand on hers*) Have I offended you?

LOUISE (*smiling without joy*) Of course not. (*She slips her hand from under his*) I am—very touched.

WALTER (*moved*) Thank you. (*Eagerly*) That is why I feel I can talk to you about Clive, for example. I am most worried for him. He is not happy now. And I do not think it is jealousy. It is something else—more deep in him—trying to explode. Like the beginning of an earthquake or so.

LOUISE (*rising and moving a step down* L) Really, my dear, don't you think you're being a little over dramatic?

WALTER (*doggedly*) No. I mean exactly this. (*He rises*) It is hard to explain.

LOUISE. I appreciate your attempt. But really, I'm sure I know my children a little better than you?

WALTER (*persisting*) Of course. But just in this case—with Clive—I feel something which frightens me—I don't know why.

LOUISE (*moving above the table; her temper breaking*) Oh, for heaven's sake . . .

(WALTER *recoils*)

(*She recovers quickly*) I mean—(*she sits above the table and pulls the newspaper towards her*) after all, as you said yourself, you *are* only a new-comer to the family. (*Sweetly*) Now, why don't you go and play me some of your nice music?

WALTER *looks confused and lowers his eyes before* LOUISE's *strained smile. He picks up his music score and exits to the kitchen.* LOUISE *sits at the head of the table staring desolately in front of her.*

CURTAIN

SCENE 2

SCENE—*The same. The same night.*

When the CURTAIN *rises, it is after supper. In the schoolroom* WALTER *is hearing* PAMELA *in her irregular verbs.* WALTER *is seated* R *of the table and* PAMELA *up* L *of it.*

PAMELA. *Je meurs, tu meurs, il meurt, nous meurons* . . .

WALTER. No.

PAMELA. It must be.

WALTER. Well it's not. *Mou* . . .

PAMELA. *Mourons.* Oh, phooey! You know, this is the perfect way to end today. It's been a stinker, hasn't it?

WALTER. Has it? I thought you had a good ride this morning.

PAMELA. Oh, that. I mean the atmosphere since I got back. What mother calls the *aura*. And Clive not coming in for lunch or dinner. D'you think he's run away?

WALTER. I think we do more French.

PAMELA. Mother was livid tonight when he didn't turn up. That's funny, too. I'd have thought daddy would have been the one to explode, but he didn't say a word. (*She leans forward, her elbows on the table*) Do you think Clive's lost his memory or something.

WALTER. What is the future of "mourir"?

PAMELA (*leaning back in her chair*) Perhaps he's been kidnapped. Just think of daddy paying ransom. I wonder if he would?

WALTER. I think Clive can take care of himself. (*He puts on his spectacles*) Now, *please*, Pamela . . .

(PAMELA *snatches the spectacles from Walter's face and puts them on her own*)

PAMELA. Oh, I'm sick of French. It's Sunday, and that's supposed to be a Day of Rest.

WALTER (*taking his spectacles from Pamela*) Yesterday you said you felt Jewish and Saturday was your Day of Rest.

PAMELA. That was Saturday—not Sunday. Today I'm going to have a hot bath and go straight to bed and read. Mary gave me a most important scientific book last week and I just haven't had a moment to glance at it.

WALTER (*suspiciously*) What kind of science?

PAMELA. Actually, it's a kind of story.

WALTER (*resigned*) Ah-ha.

PAMELA. But completely scientific. It tells what would happen if the earth got invaded by Venus. The people are just sweeties. They're all ten foot high and covered with blue jelly.

WALTER. Very educational.

(LOUISE *enters on the landing from* R. *She is rather strained and anxious*)

LOUISE (*calling*) Pamela—Pamela. (*She goes up the stairs to the schoolroom*)

PAMELA. There you are. You can't even have a scientific discussion any more without being interrupted by the world of triviality.

(LOUISE *comes into the schoolroom.* WALTER *rises and stands uncomfortably by the table*)

LOUISE (*to Pamela*) How's the bruise, darling? I've turned on your bath.

PAMELA. Has Clive turned up yet?

LOUISE (*wearily, but with a vestige of deep anger*) No, not yet. (*She softens*) Now, get into your bath and don't dawdle about in here. (*Having virtually ignored Walter, she just notices him as she turns to go*) Good night, Walter.

WALTER. Good night, Mrs Harrington.

(LOUISE *goes down the stairs into the hall, takes a wool stole from the pegs, puts it on then exits by the front door to look for Clive.* PAMELA *rises and looks down the stairs*)

PAMELA (*whispering*) She looks as if she needs a fizzy.

WALTER. Ssh. Tch-tch! (*He resumes his seat*)

PAMELA (*turning to Walter*) Well, she does. Mother always goes like that when she's lost an argument. It's meant to mean she's been misunderstood.

WALTER (*putting on his spectacles*) She is worried about Clive.

PAMELA (*leaning over the back of her chair*) Phooey! Anyone would think he was still a baby, the way she goes on. (*She straightens up. Wickedly*) I hope he stays out all night. Wouldn't it be wonderful if he was giving babies to all the schoolgirls in Ipswich? (*In an affected voice*) Well, I'd better go and have a bath, dear boy.

> (PAMELA *exits to her bedroom.*
>
> LOUISE *enters by the front door, goes into the living-room, switches on the lights* R, *crosses and exits by the french windows, leaving the windows open.*
>
> PAMELA *enters from her bedroom carrying her dressing-gown, nightdress and slippers*)

Oh, Lord, Sunday night. Breakfast at half past seven for that rotten train. (*She goes down the schoolroom stairs*) I think Mondays stink. (*She runs back up the stairs to the schoolroom*) Is there any religion with its Day of Rest on Mondays?

WALTER. Yes, the religion of Lazy Girls.

PAMELA. Oh, you are brutish!

> (PAMELA *goes down to the landing and exits* R. WALTER *gets a book from the shelves, sits and reads.*
>
> STANLEY *enters by the front door and removes his hat and mackintosh.*
>
> LOUISE *enters by the french windows and hears Stanley*)

LOUISE (*calling*) Clive?

> (STANLEY *appears at the living-room door*)

Oh, it's you. (*She closes the french windows and curtains*)

STANLEY (*hanging his hat and mackintosh on the hall pegs*) Isn't he back?

LOUISE. No.

STANLEY (*coming into the living-room*) Well, no-one's seen him in the village. He hasn't been in any of the pubs.

LOUISE (*bitterly*) The pubs. Always the pubs.

STANLEY. Well, where else would he be likely to go? (*He sits on the coffee-table*) You know what the trouble is? Your son's turning into a drunkard.

LOUISE (*removing her stole and putting it over the back of the chair* L *of the table*) The way you've been behaving lately's enough to make anyone drink. (*She crosses and sits in the armchair*) No-one would think he's your son. You treat him abominably.

STANLEY. Do I?

LOUISE. You haven't the faintest idea how to deal with sensitive people. If I was Clive, I'd have run away from home long ago.

STANLEY (*bitterly*) If it weren't for the saving grace of his mother. His sensitive mother.

LOUISE. At least I understand him. I make an effort. Just because you can't see beyond the end of your stupid, commonplace nose . . .

STANLEY (*rising; savagely*) Shut up! (*He goes to the sideboard and noisily pours himself a whisky and soda*)

LOUISE. Charming!

STANLEY (*his pain also becoming rage*) And what have you done for him that's so wonderful, may I ask? (*He moves up L of Louise*) I'll tell you. Turned him into a snivelling little neurotic. A mother's boy.

LOUISE (*trying to recover poise*) That's not true.

STANLEY. And I'll tell you something else. He's going peculiar. Yes—looney, if you want to know. He talked to me last night and I didn't understand one word he said.

LOUISE (*loftily*) That doesn't surprise me.

STANLEY. It was like listening to a lunatic.

LOUISE. And that's my fault, too? Just because I take an interest in our son, which you've never bothered to do in all these years, I'm driving him insane.

STANLEY (*crossing above Louise to the sofa; with wild demand in his tone*) And when I tried to teach him things, what happened?

LOUISE. What things?

STANLEY. Golf—swimming—I don't know, I can't remember. Who was it said, "Clive's too delicate. Clive can't waste his time on silly games. He's got his reading to do." (*He sits on the sofa*)

LOUISE. So it was wrong of me to encourage his reading?

STANLEY. He was my son as much as yours.

LOUISE. Yes, and what did you want to do for him? Push him straight into your third-rate furniture business for the rest of his life. Well, that's not good enough for *me*, Stanley.

STANLEY (*cutting through this*) He was my son.

LOUISE. He still *is*.

STANLEY (*hard*) No. Not any more. You've seen to that.

(LOUISE *looks sharply away from him*)

LOUISE (*collected*) That's the nastiest thing you've ever said to me.

STANLEY. I didn't mean it.

LOUISE. Yes, you did.

STANLEY (*wearily*) I don't know what I mean any more. It's all so bloody mixed up.

LOUISE. Must you swear?

STANLEY. *I* don't know . . .

LOUISE. I can't stand much more of this. (*She rises and moves above the armchair*) I just can't.

STANLEY (*dead*) What?

LOUISE. It's no good, Stanley. (*She moves to* R *of the armchair*) My life was never meant to be like this—limited this way. I know I'm unpredictable sometimes. I say things I don't mean. But don't you see I'm just so frustrated, I don't know what I'm doing half the time? I'm sorry, but it's the only word, Stanley. (*She moves to* L *of the sofa*) There are times I feel I'm being choked to death—suffocated under piles of English blankets. Yes, my dear. I'm not English and won't ever be, no matter how hard I try. Can't you ever understand that you married someone who's really a Parisian at heart? A Frenchwoman, my dear man, with all that means—faults, too, of course—frivolity and being irresponsible. If I've disappointed you, it's because I've never really become *acclimatee*—you know, acclimatized—that's all. I've never been able to take your world of shops and business seriously. Can't you understand? (*She moves and sits in the armchair*) Can't you understand anything at all?

STANLEY (*flat*) What do you want me to do, Louise? (*He pauses*) Louise, I'm asking you a question. D'you want a divorce? (*He pauses*) Well?

LOUISE. Oh, it's all so vulgar.

STANLEY (*tired*) I'm a vulgar man.

LOUISE. Do *you*? Do *you* want one?

STANLEY (*plainly*) I'm too old to start again.

LOUISE. That's a nice way of putting it.

STANLEY. Oh, for heaven's sake—*nice!* And besides, there's Pam. It wouldn't do her any good.

LOUISE. I notice you don't even mention Clive.

STANLEY. Clive's no longer a child. Although it probably upsets you to think of it, he's almost twenty years old.

LOUISE. I think it's you who haven't gathered that.

STANLEY. Don't start—just don't start.

LOUISE. I didn't begin it.

STANLEY (*rising; frantic*) Louise . . . (*He pauses and moves up* R *of the armchair. In an altered voice; not looking at her*) Do you think if we went away it would help? Just the two of us, alone together? We could go back to Monte.

LOUISE. You know I can't stand the place.

(PAMELA *enters on the landing from* R *and goes down to the hall. She wears her dressing-gown and slippers*)

STANLEY (*moving to the sideboard; controlling himself*) Well, anywhere . . .

(PAMELA *comes into the living-room*)

LOUISE. Clive? Oh, it's you, Pam.

PAMELA. Yes, Mother. Isn't Clive back yet?

LOUISE. No—not yet.

PAMELA. I've had a lovely bath and I'm going to bed.

LOUISE. Good night, darling.

(PAMELA *kisses Louise*)

And don't read too late.

PAMELA. Good night. (*She moves to Stanley*) Good night, Daddy. (*She kisses Stanley, moves to the hall door, pauses a moment, turns, looks silently at Louise and Stanley then goes into the hall and up the stairs to the schoolroom*)

STANLEY (*crossing and sitting on the sofa*) It's worth a try, isn't it, Louise?

LOUISE. Yes, Stanley. It is worth a try.

PAMELA (*to Walter*) Good night.

WALTER. Sleep tight.

(LOUISE *takes a cigarette from the box on the stool* R *of her chair and lights it*)

PAMELA. Mind the bugs don't bite.

(PAMELA *exits to her bedroom*)

LOUISE (*after a pause; lightly and without an obvious sense of calculation*) Stanley—(*she rises and moves up* R) I want to ask you to do something for me—(*she turns to him*) something rather difficult.

STANLEY. What's that?

LOUISE (*moving to* L *of him*) It's to do with Pamela. I feel it's something you can manage better than I can.

STANLEY. Pam?

LOUISE (*turning and moving up* L *of the armchair*) Actually, it's about Walter. I'm afraid he's having rather a bad effect on her. She's just at that stage, you know—impressionable, romantic— long walks in the moonlight. Well, I'm afraid she's got a bit of a crush. Nothing serious, of course—she'll soon get over it.

STANLEY. You want me to talk to her?

LOUISE. No. Something rather more drastic, I'm afraid. I think we must let Walter go. In the most tactful way, of course. (*She moves up* R *of the armchair*) But I do think the sooner the better.

STANLEY. I see.

LOUISE (*moving to the hall door*) He's upstairs, now—shall I ask him to come down? (*She opens the door*) Then I'll make myself scarce. (*With a step towards Stanley*) But you will be very tactful, won't you?

(CLIVE *blunders in by the front door. He is drunk, but, as on the previous evening, perfectly coherent*)

She sees Clive and moves a little L) Clive!

(CLIVE *comes into the living-room and crosses below Louise to the armchair*)

CLIVE (*as he enter   Good evening, all.

STANLEY (*rising*) Would you mind telling me where you've been? (*He pauses*) Did you hear me? You've been out since twelve.

CLIVE (*slumping into the armchair*) Like the tide. But we're back, you see.

(LOUISE *moves up* R *of the armchair*)

STANLEY (*with a step towards Clive*) Answer me!

CLIVE. Why the hell do we always have to ask expected questions?

STANLEY (*moving to* R *of Clive*) Now listen, my boy, you've been drin . . .

LOUISE (*interrupting; quietly*) Stanley, why don't you go upstairs and do what I asked?

STANLEY. Very well. I'll leave you to take care of your sensitive son. (*He looks angrily at Clive for a moment, then goes briskly into the hall, closes the door behind him and goes up to the landing*)

LOUISE (*moving to* R *of Clive; bitterly*) Your father and I have been worried to death.

CLIVE (*insolently*) Do I detect a new note in the air? Your father and I. How splendid! The birth of a new moral being. Your-father-and-I. When did you last see your-father-and-I? Or is it just a new alliance? All the same, I congratulate you. I always thought you two ought to get married.

(STANLEY *knocks at the door of Walter's room, and receiving no reply, goes less resolutely up the stairs to the schoolroom*)

LOUISE. You're drunk! And disgusting! You'd better go to bed. (*She crosses to the kitchen door*) I'll get you something to eat.

CLIVE (*looking round at Louise; coldly*) Your-father-and-I will now get your supper.

(LOUISE *reacts then exits to the kitchen. The lights trouble* CLIVE *who rises, shuffles clumsily to the switch* R *and switches off the bracket, leaving only the glow from the fire spot in the footlights. He returns to the armchair, sinks wearily into it and covers his eyes.* STANLEY *enters the schoolroom and closes the curtain behind him.* WALTER *rises, as always, made nervous by Stanley's appearance*)

STANLEY. Are you busy?

WALTER. Of course not, Mr Harrington. I was just reading. Is Clive back yet?

STANLEY. He just came in—drunk. Do you drink? I don't remember seeing you.

WALTER. Not very much, no.

STANLEY. Sensible. (*He pauses*) My son drinks. A lot. Doesn't he?

(WALTER *is silent*)

Why does he drink? (*He sits* L *of the table*) Can you see any good reason for it? What?

WALTER. I do not think people drink for good reasons.

STANLEY. Sit down.

(WALTER *sits uneasily* R *of the table*)

You don't think much of me, do you?

WALTER. Mr Harrington . . .

STANLEY. Why? Because I'm not educated. Is that it?

WALTER. Of course not.

STANLEY. Then why? Because the children say things?

WALTER. Mr Harrington, please, I . . .

STANLEY. And what do they know? People say parents are selfish. They've got nothing on children. Do children ever think about anything but themselves? *Their* troubles? As if nobody ever had 'em before. Well? You ought to know. You teach 'em.

WALTER (*softly*) I think children are not so able to help themselves with their troubles.

STANLEY (*not really listening*) I tell you, children are the most selfish things in the world. So he drinks. Did you know it was my fault? I drive him to it. So I hear.

(WALTER *is silent*)

Well? Have you lost your tongue?

WALTER (*in a very low voice*) No.

STANLEY. I'll tell you why he drinks. So he can get over being with me. Have you noticed how this family of mine never get together in this house? Are you afraid of me?

WALTER (*straight*) No.

STANLEY. Well, that's a wonder. My son is. That's something else I hear. What do you think?

WALTER. I think—yes.

STANLEY (*blankly*) Do you?

WALTER (*with difficulty*) I think he feels you do not love him, but still are expecting him to love you.

STANLEY. Rubbish!

WALTER. I'm sorry. You did ask me.

STANLEY. He's my *son*. How can he think that?

WALTER. Perhaps he does not—does not wish to be alone with you, because he feels often you are—well—judging him. When you look at him, he sees you are thinking, "How useless he is."

STANLEY. And when he looks at me—what's *he* thinking? Ah, that's a different story, isn't it? (*Bitterly*) "How common he is."

WALTER. Oh, no . . .

STANLEY. Don't tell me. Common! I've seen it too often.

WALTER (*overbearing him urgently*) No! You are wrong about him. You see, in front of you he must always justify his life. His

Greek, maybe, or because he loves an opera. When a boy must apologize for ears and eyes, it is very bad.

STANLEY. Apologize? When have I asked him to apologize?

WALTER. That's not what I mean.

STANLEY. Then why use such ridiculous words? I can see now where he gets them from.

WALTER (*gravely*) Your son has got nothing from me. I wish he had. Mr Harrington, your son needs help. Will he get it?

STANLEY. He can always come to me. He knows that.

WALTER (*raising his voice slightly*) And will he come? *Does* he come?

STANLEY (*gathering dignity about him*) As a matter of fact, we had a very frank talk last night. You didn't know that, did you? (*He pauses*) What are you thinking?

WALTER. You know you are very like your son, Mr Harrington.

STANLEY (*sarcastically*) Oh, yes. In education, I suppose?

WALTER. I say too much always.

(STANLEY *shrugs and suddenly he begins to talk more or less to himself*)

STANLEY. What's it matter? You start a family, work and plan. Suddenly you turn round and there's nothing there. Probably never was. What's a family, anyway? Just—just kids with your blood in 'em. There's no reason why they should like you. You go on expecting it, of course, but it's silly, really. Like expecting 'em to know what they meant to you when they were babies. They're not supposed to know, perhaps. It's not natural, really, when you come to think of it. You can't expect anybody to know what they mean to somebody else—it's not the way of things. (*He stops, confused. When he resumes his voice is even softer*) There's just nothing. Bloody nothing.

(WALTER, *unseen by Stanley, gestures towards him in a futile attempt at communication*)

(*He goes on staring into space, not heeding Walter at all*) You get a wife and family and you work for them. And all the time you think: "It'll be better next year. Next year it'll be all right." The children going to prep school, leaving it. Short trousers, long trousers. Perhaps he'll make the rugger fifteen or the cricket team or something—anything—and then his first girl friend and taking her home—or perhaps just keeping her to himself till he's sure. (*Frankly*) But nothing—nothing. And now he hates me.

WALTER. No.

STANLEY (*focusing again*) D'you think I don't know? How sensitive do you have to be for that? Tell me, because I don't know too much about that sort of thing—(*his bitterness rises again*) I'm always too busy making money. (*Violently*) Go on, tell me.

Sensitive people have deep feelings, don't they? They suffer a lot.

WALTER, Please, Mr Harrington . . .

STANLEY (*banging the table with his fist; violently*) I don't want to hear.

WALTER (*rising*) Excuse me, sir.

(WALTER, *bewildered, goes down the stairs, hesitates for a moment on the landing, then continues to the hall and goes into the living-room. STANLEY rises, moves to the window and stares out. The lights in the schoolroom fade to a half.* CLIVE, *in the living-room, is lying inert in the armchair in a strange awkward position suggesting acute depression. The lights around the armchair area come up a little*)

(*He closes the door and stands behind the armchair*) Clive? What's the matter? Are you all right? Why are you sitting in the dark?

(STANLEY *sits* R *of the table, facing up stage with his head on his hand*)

I've been talking to your father. He thinks you hate him.

(CLIVE *does not appear to hear*)

Clive, listen to me. The Kings of Egypt were gods. Everything they did was right, everything they said was true, everyone they loved became important. And when they died, they grew faces of gold. You must try to forgive your parents for being average and wrong when you worshipped them once. Why are you so afraid? (*He moves down* R *of Clive*) Is it—because you have no girl friend? (*He sits on the stool,* R *of Clive*) Oh, you are so silly. Silly. Do you think sex will change you? Put you into a different world, where everything will mean more to you? I thought so, too, once. I thought it would change me into a man so my father could never touch me again. I didn't know exactly what it would be like, but I thought it would burn me and bring me terrible pain. But afterwards, I'd be strong and very wise. There was a girl in Muhlbach. She worked in her mother's grocery shop. One night I had a few drinks and, just for a joke, I broke into her bedroom through the window. I stayed with her all night. And I entered heaven. I really did. Between her arms was the only place in the world that mattered. When daylight came, I felt I had changed for ever. A little later I got up. I looked round, but the room was exactly the same. This was incomprehensible. It should have been so huge now—filled with air. But it seemed very small and stuffy and outside it was raining. I suppose I had thought, "Now it will never rain again," because rain depresses me, and I was now a man and could not be depressed. I remember, I hated the soap for lying there in the dish just as it had done the night before. I watched her putting on her clothes. I thought: "We're tied to-gether now by an invisible thread." And then she said: "It's nine o'clock: I must be off"—and went downstairs to open the shop. Then I looked into the mirror: at least my eyes would be different. (*Ironically*) They were a little red, yes—but I was exactly the same—still a boy. Rain was still here. And all the problems of yesterday were still waiting. (*He pauses and puts his hand on Clive's arm*) Sex by itself is nothing, believe me. Just like breathing—only important when it goes wrong. And Clive, this only happens if you're afraid of it. What are you thinking? (*He pauses*) Please talk to me.

CLIVE (*in a very low voice*) Walter.

WALTER. Yes?

CLIVE (*his head buried*) What's wrong with me?

WALTER. There's nothing wrong with you. Nothing.

CLIVE. Don't fool me. I know.

WALTER. There's nothing wrong but in your mind. What you think about.

CLIVE (*despairing*) What is it? What have they done to me?

WALTER. Clive—your parents love you. Everything they have done has been from love. I am sure of this.

CLIVE. Then God save me from love.

WALTER. He will not. You have more in you than any man I've ever met.

CLIVE (*breaking free*) Stop it . . .

WALTER. Clive, my dear friend, let me help you.

CLIVE. Cut that out!

WALTER. What?

CLIVE. Pity. Do you think I'd have let him take the guts out of me, if his attempts to love me weren't so rotten to watch?

WALTER (*gently*) I don't pity you, Clive. And you mustn't pity yourself. You can end this and you must. You must leave here. You—not me. At the moment you are—(*he gestures*) on your family. I don't know the word. Like a butterfly on a pin.

CLIVE (*with distaste*) Impaled.

WALTER. Yes. And you must get off the pin. At the end of term in Cambridge, don't come back here. Go anywhere else you like. Join your American friend singing. Go into a factory. Anything. The important thing is this—as soon as you are out of here, people will start telling you who you are. (*Tenderly*) Maybe you will not like it, but that's nonsense—you must always like the truth.

(CLIVE *shakes his head*)

You think you can't do this, but you must. Oh, is this so difficult? I could tell you what *I* want. To live in England. To be happy teaching. One day to marry. To have children, and many English friends. And now you. What do *you* want?

CLIVE (*faintly*) Something—I'm not sure. (*Intimately*) Yes—I think I want—to achieve something that only I could do, no-one else. I want to fall in love with just one person. To know what it is to bless and be blessed.

(STANLEY *begins to come out of his reverie*)

And to serve a great cause with devotion. (*Appealing*) I want to be *involved*.

(STANLEY *rises, moves to the schoolroom door, switches off the light, goes down to the hall and stands for a few moments outside the living-room door, listening*)

WALTER. Then break the glass. Get out of the coffin. Trust everything, not because it's wise, but because not to trust will kill you. Trust me, for instance. I'll see you often. But you must go away from here. Say, "Yes—you will go."

(STANLEY *comes unheard into the living-room and stands* L *of the screen, still listening*)

CLIVE (*nodding*) Yes. I'll go.
WALTER. The next vacation?
CLIVE. The next vacation.
WALTER. Good!
CLIVE. Isn't it silly? We seem to spend all the time ordering each other out of the house.
WALTER. A very friendly way to spend the time.

(STANLEY *switches on the lights.* WALTER *looks round and rises*)

STANLEY (*crossing above the armchair to* L *of it*) Clive—don't you think it's time you went to bed?
CLIVE (*rising*) I suppose so. (*He crosses below Walter to the hall door*)
WALTER (*to Clive as he passes; gently*) You're sure you are all right, now?
CLIVE (*looking back from the doorway*) Yes, I'm all right.

(CLIVE *moves into the hall, closes the door then goes up the stairs and exits on the landing to* R. WALTER *looks at his watch, gives his half bow to Stanley and moves towards the hall door*)

STANLEY (*raging*) Just who the hell do you think you are?
WALTER (*stopping and turning*) I'm sorry?
STANLEY. The world owes you a living—that's it.
WALTER. Mr Harrington . . .
STANLEY (*brutally*) Don't "Mr Harrington" me, with your smarmy voice and bowing from the waist. You had the gall to patronize me just now—tell me what's wrong with my home . . .
WALTER. You forget—you asked me for my opinion.
STANLEY. Oh, yes. And what else did I ask you to do? (*He moves to* L *of Walter*) Turn my son into a cissy?

WALTER (*retreating below the armchair*) Your son is a fine, intelligent boy.

(STANLEY *follows* WALTER *who retreats to* L *of the armchair*)

STANLEY. He's a mess, that's what he is. And it's your fault.

WALTER (*turning to him*) My fault?

STANLEY (*blindly*) Yes, yours. *Yours.* You, the arty boys. It's you who've taken him. (*He hurls the following names as if they were insults*) Shakespeare! Beethoven! All the time, till I can't touch him. What gave you the right to steal my boy?

WALTER (*turning away* L; *with pity*) You will believe what you please.

STANLEY (*crossing to* R *of Walter*) I'm not blind, you know—and I'm not deaf. I heard you telling him just now—"Get out of this house," you said.

WALTER (*turning to face Stanley*) Yes, I did.

STANLEY. How dare you say a thing like that? What right have you—in my house, working for me—to say a thing like that?

WALTER. My friendship for your son.

STANLEY. Oh, of course! And your friendship with my daughter, Pamela, too—what about that?

WALTER. Pamela?

STANLEY (*crisply; with satisfaction*) Your employer, Mrs Harrington, has asked me to dismiss you because she thinks you are having a bad effect upon our daughter.

WALTER (*after a pause*) Mrs Harrington said this?

STANLEY. Yes.

WALTER. But it's not true. Not true at all.

STANLEY (*carefully*) No. I don't think it is.

(*There is a slight pause.* WALTER *looks in utter distress and bewilderment at Stanley*)

WALTER. Then—why?

STANLEY. Could it be because you've been trying to make love to my wife?

(WALTER *reacts sharply to protest*)

You filthy German bastard.

(WALTER *winces as if he has been slapped*)

Once a German, always a German. Take what you want and the hell with everyone else.

(WALTER *stands rigid, with his face averted*)

You're a fool, too. Did you really think my wife would ever risk anything for you? Oh, I know it's very cultured to look down on money, but that's a very different thing from giving it up. Well, now, you've had your chips, and she's sent me to give them to you. (*He turns and sits in the armchair*)

(*There is a long pause.* WALTER *crosses above Stanley towards the hall door, then stops and turns back to* R *of him. When he speaks, it is very quietly, from the depth of his humiliation*)

WALTER. You can't believe this? It's not possible.

STANLEY. Oh, yes—it's quite possible. I've got a perfect witness: "unimpeachable", as we say in England.

(WALTER *looks at him*)

Can't you guess? No? (*Hard*) Your pal. Your good pal.

WALTER (*whispering*) Clive?

STANLEY. Of course, Clive: who else?

WALTER (*in disbelief*) No!

STANLEY. He told me he saw you both—in this room, last night.

WALTER. No—oh, no—but . . .

STANLEY. Do you know what we do with people like you in England? Chuck 'em out. (*He lowers his voice*) I'm going to fix it so you never get your naturalization papers. I'm going to write to the immigration people. I'll write tonight, and tell them all about you. I'll say—let's see: "Much though I hate to complain about people behind their backs, I feel it my duty in this case to warn you about this young German's standard of morality. Whilst under my roof, he attempted to force his attentions on my young daughter, who is only fourteen." Try to get your papers after that. They'll send you back to the place where you belong.

(LOUISE *enters from the kitchen carrying a tray with a plate of sandwiches and a beaker of milk*)

LOUISE (*putting the tray on the sideboard*) Stanley, I thought you were upstairs. Where's Clive? (*She moves up* R *of the armchair*) Walter! What's the matter?

STANLEY. I did what you asked me.

LOUISE. Yes, but *how* did you do it? (*She moves to Walter*) Was he very brutal, *mon cher*?

(WALTER *does not look at Louise*)

But you know yourself it's for the best, don't you? (*She touches Walter's arm*) So it's foolish to be upset. Walter, please.

(WALTER *falls on his knees and grasps Louise's hand in an imploring, desperate, filial gesture*)

WALTER. Don't—I beg of you . . .

(STANLEY *rises and backs away from them, up* L *of the table, watching them all the time*)

LOUISE (*trying to free herself; extremely ruffled*) Let go my hands!
WALTER. No—please. No.
LOUISE. Walter—get up at once.
WALTER. Please—don't . . .
LOUISE. Do you hear me?

(STANLEY *moves* L *of the table*)

Will you stop making an exhibition of yourself? You're embarrassing and ridiculous. (*She breaks from Walter and moves up* L
of the armchair) Now, get up.

(WALTER *rises and stands facing away from Louise*)

I'm sorry, but I'm afraid you deserved to be spoken to like that.
I'm really very disappointed in you. Both our children have been
considerably disturbed by your presence in our house. And, of
course, my husband and I could never allow that. They have
always come first with me as I'm sure you understand.

(WALTER *is silent*)

Now, about the financial arrangements, we will make it as easy
for you as possible. (*She turns to Stanley*) You could manage an
extra month's wages, I think, Stanley?
STANLEY. Oh—yes.
LOUISE (*turning to Walter*) There you are. I call that quite
generous, don't you?
WALTER (*in a remote, disinterested voice*) Yes.
LOUISE (*with a step towards Walter; seeing his distress*) Oh, Hibou,
please don't look so stricken. It makes it so much more difficult
for everybody.

(WALTER *turns abruptly, goes into the hall and up to the landing,
where he leans against the wall for a moment, with his eyes closed.*
LOUISE *gazes for a moment after Walter, then moves quickly to the
foot of the stairs.*
    CLIVE *enters on the landing from* R *and sees Walter*)

CLIVE. Walter—what's the matter?
WALTER. No!

(WALTER *rushes into his room and closes the door.* LOUISE *goes into
the sitting-room, closes the door and crosses to Stanley.* CLIVE *pauses
a moment outside Walter's room, then goes down to the hall*)

LOUISE (*to Stanley*) Well, of all the embarrassing, hysterical
scenes. You certainly seem to have handled things brilliantly.

(CLIVE *comes into the living-room, leaving the door open*)

CLIVE (*standing by the screen*) What's the matter with Walter?
LOUISE (*transferring the tray to the upstage end of the table*) He's

a little upset. There's some supper here for you—you'd better eat it. (*She moves to the sideboard*)

CLIVE. Why is he upset? What's been going on down here?

LOUISE (*turning to Clive*) I think it's better if we don't talk about it. (*She turns to the sideboard and noisily tidies the things on it*)

CLIVE (*crossing down L of the table*) Do you want to talk about it, Father? (*He pauses*) Father—I'm asking you a question. Do you hear me?

LOUISE (*moving up R of the table*) Don't be so impertinent, Clive—speaking to your father like that.

CLIVE. Ah—your-father-and-I—the new alliance. What have you done to Walter, *both* of you? (*He pauses*)

(LOUISE *and* STANLEY *exchange a look, then* LOUISE *turns away and crosses to* L *of the sofa*)

I'm only asking a simple question.

STANLEY (*moving slowly above the table*) If you really want to know, I told him what you said last night about him and your mother.

LOUISE (*turning quickly to Stanley*) Me?

STANLEY (*moving up L of the armchair*) You and your daughter's tutor, my dear—a pretty picture.

LOUISE (*with a step towards Stanley*) What did he tell you? What did he say?

STANLEY. Never mind—I didn't believe it.

LOUISE. I want to know what Clive said to you.

STANLEY. What's it matter? It never matters what he says.

CLIVE (*moving down R of the bench*) So you didn't believe me?

(LOUISE *sinks on to the sofa at the left end*)

STANLEY. Did you really think I would?

CLIVE. Then why did you talk to Walter just now as if you did? Why was he so upset? Well?

(STANLEY *is past reply, justification, or even the attitude of parenthood. Without answering, he moves into the hall, closes the door behind him, goes up the stairs and exits on the landing to* R)

(*He moves slowly above the armchair and stands up* R *of it*) Well, Mother?

LOUISE. Jou-Jou—Jou-Jou, you didn't suggest . . . ? (*She glances away from Clive to the right end of the sofa where Walter had sat, then looks at Clive*) But this is horrible. You couldn't have said such things about me, surely?

CLIVE. Yes—I said them.

LOUISE. But why?

CLIVE. I don't know.

LOUISE. Jou-Jou!

CLIVE (*turning away a step*) I don't know. (*He turns to Louise*) I

do something terrible that I'll remember all my life, that'll make
me sick whenever I think of it—(*he moves up* L *of the armchair*) and
I don't know why.

LOUISE. You're ill—you must be.

CLIVE. Oh, no. It only means *I* can damage people, too—
that's all. I can dish it out—just like everyone else.

LOUISE (*rising and crossing to Clive*) But it's not true. It's not
true, what you said.

CLIVE. True? I told the lie, yes. But what I felt under the lie—
about you and Walter—was that so untrue?

LOUISE. Clive, you must listen . . .

CLIVE (*moving down* R) No, don't answer because whatever you
said wouldn't be real. You've forgotten what it is to be honest
about feeling. True! The only true thing I know is what's happened to him—my father.

LOUISE (*moving down* L *of the armchair*) You must be out of your
mind.

CLIVE. Yes—and you're so worried about me. Department of
Flattering Unction.

LOUISE (*moving below the armchair*) Clive—you frighten me. Why
are you being so terrible? What have I done?

CLIVE. Don't you know? Can't you *see* what you've done?
There isn't a Stanley Harrington any more. We've broken him in
bits between us.

LOUISE (*sitting in the armchair*) I don't know what you're talking
about. I don't . . .

CLIVE. No—you don't. Poor man.

LOUISE. Clive—you hate me.

CLIVE. I hate. Isn't that enough? (*He moves up* R *of the armchair.
After a pause*) Is the war in this house never going to end?

LOUISE. War? What war?

CLIVE. The war you both declared when you married. The
culture war with me as ammunition. (*He moves down* R) "Let's
show him how small he is. Let's show her where she gets off."
And always through me. He wasn't always a bully. (*He moves up* R
of the armchair) You made him into one.

LOUISE (*rising and moving to* R *of the bench*) I'll not go on with
this conversation another moment. It's obscene. Your father's
upset. Simply upset, that's all.

CLIVE. But *why* is he upset?

LOUISE. About something I asked him to do.

CLIVE. It was something to do with Walter, wasn't it? What
have you done to Walter?

LOUISE. If you must know—he's been dismissed.

CLIVE. Mother—no!

LOUISE. I assure you there were excellent reasons.

CLIVE. But you can't dismiss him. You *can't*. Not even you.
(*In sudden despair*) He can't go away from here.

(LOUISE *looks anxiously at Clive*)

LOUISE (*calmly*) I did it because of Pamela. I'm afraid his influence over her was getting rather stronger than I cared for.

(*The opening of the slow Third Movement of Mahler's Symphony Number Four in G Major is heard from the gramophone in Walter's room.* LOUISE, *hearing the music, reacts*)

CLIVE (*after a pause; calmly*) I see.

LOUISE (*crossing to the coffee-table* R) Well, evidently the boy himself is not so shattered by the news as you are. (*She sits on the downstage side of the coffee-table, facing front*) Don't you think you'd better eat your supper?

CLIVE (*matter-of-fact*) What was it? Jealousy? Shame, when you saw them so innocent together? Or just the sheer vulgarity of competing with one's own daughter?

LOUISE (*turning to face Clive*) How dare you!

CLIVE. Dearest Mother, who are you trying to fool? I know your rules. Don't give sympathy to a man if others are giving it, too—he'll never see how unique *you* are. Besides, doing what everyone else does is just too vulgar. Like going to Monte, or falling in love.

(LOUISE *bursts into tears*)

(*Anguished*) Mother!

(LOUISE *sobs helplessly for a moment*)

(*With a wild, hopeless grief*) Oh, it goes on and on. No meeting. Never. Why can't we be important to each other? Why can't we ever come back into the room and be new to each other? Why doesn't a night's sleep, lying all those dark hours with ourselves forgotten and then coming alive again, why doesn't it ever change us? Give us new things to see—new things to say, too, not just "Eat your eggs" or "You were in late"—the old dreariness. (*To Louise. Desperately*) I want to *know* you. But you wonderful— changed into yourself. Don't you understand? So that you can change me.

(LOUISE *sits unmoving, no longer crying and giving no indication of having heard*)

(*He kneels and embraces Louise with desperate tenderness*) Maman— Maman, *cherie* . . .

(LOUISE *endures Clive's embrace for a moment then with a slow, cold gesture, pushes him away*)

LOUISE. Don't!

CLIVE (*falling back*) Maman! (*He sits on the floor, leaning back on his hands, which are flat on the floor behind him*)

LOUISE (*rounding on him; her face terrible*) D'you think you're the only one can ask terrible questions? Supposing I ask a few. Supposing I ask them. You ought to be glad Walter's going, but you're not. Why not? Why aren't you glad? You want him to stay, don't you? You want him to stay very much. Why?

(CLIVE *rises and backs a step* L, *staring at Louise*)

CLIVE (*in a panic*) Maman . . .

(*The gramophone record sticks. The passage is repeated again and again. The needle is not moved on*)

LOUISE (*harsh and pitiless*) Why? You said filthy things to your father about me. Filth and lies. Why? Can you think of an answer? Why, Clive? Why about me and Walter? (*She rises and moves to* .R *of the armchair*) Why? (*She moves behind the armchair*) Why? Why?

CLIVE (*in a scream*) You're *killing* . . . (*He backs* L, *turns and falls on one knee on the bench with his arms and body across the table*)

(*In the silence following Clive's collapse, the repeated passage on the record is clearly heard four times.*

STANLEY *enters on the landing from* R *and thumps on Walter's door.* LOUISE *and* CLIVE *become aware of the noise. They both turn sharply* R *to listen.* STANLEY, *receiving no answer from Walter, turns the handle but has to push the door hard to get it open as Walter's jacket is stuffed under it.* STANLEY, *coughing from the gas in Walter's room, picks up the jacket so that it is clearly seen by the audience. He throws the jacket on the floor and exits to Walter's room. He re-enters almost immediately and rushes to the top of the stairs.* LOUISE *crosses to the hall door and opens it*)

STANLEY (*calling*) Louise. Louise.
LOUISE. Stanley? (*She runs up to the landing*)
STANLEY. Get the doctor.

(STANLEY *exits to Walter's room. The record is switched off*)

LOUISE. What is it?

(LOUISE *exits to Walter's room*)

(*Off*) What's happened?
STANLEY (*off*) It's Walter! Get a doctor! Quick!

(LOUISE *re-enters, coughing from the gas, and goes down to the hall.* CLIVE *rises and crosses slowly to the hall door.* LOUISE *goes to the telephone and lifts the receiver*)

LOUISE (*into the telephone*) Hello . . . Hello . . . Three-four-two, please . . . (*She waits and remains at the telephone until the end of the Act*)

(CLIVE *goes into the hall and up the stairs.*

STANLEY *enters from Walter's room, dragging the unconscious* WALTER *with him. He lowers Walter gently to the landing floor*)

STANLEY (*kneeling over the body; rapidly and urgently*) Dear God, let him live! Dear God, let him live—please—dear God—I'll never . . .

(CLIVE *reaches the landing and kneels by Walter, next to Stanley*)

CLIVE. Walter!

(WALTER *stirs*)

STANLEY. He's all right! He's all right!
WALTER. *Schon gut. Mir fehlt nichts.*
STANLEY (*joyfully*) Thank God! Boy! (*He hugs Walter to him*)

(PAMELA *enters the schoolroom from her bedroom, pulling on her dressing-gown. She switches on the schoolroom light.* CLIVE *rises, runs up the stairs into the schoolroom and closes the entrance curtain.* STANLEY *slowly loosens Walter's collar*)

PAMELA. What is it? What's the matter?
CLIVE. Nothing. It's all right. It's all right. Walter fell down and hurt himself. Like you did. Now, go back to bed. (*Kindly*) Go on. (*He pushes Pamela gently to her bedroom*)

(PAMELA *exits to her bedroom, and* CLIVE *closes the door. The lights slowly fade on the living-room, then on the landing*)

(*He faces the window; urgently*) The courage. For all of us. Oh, God —*give* it.

CURTAIN

FURNITURE AND PROPERTY LIST

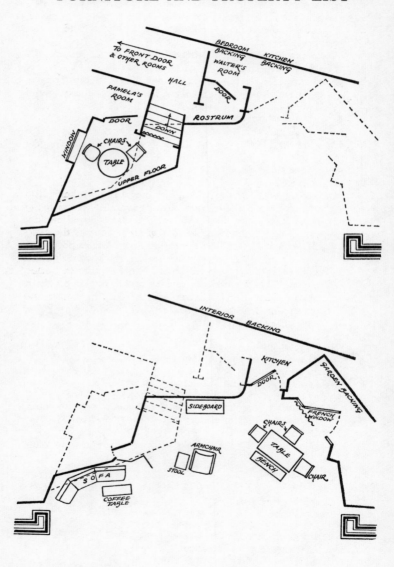

ACT I

SCENE I

On stage: *In the living-room:* banquette or sofa. *On it:* cushions
              Low coffee-table. *On it:* box with cigarettes, jar of tobacco,
                 table-lighter, ashtray, matches, packet of cigarettes
              Folding screen
              Large pottery vase. *In it:* Michaelmas daisies
              Contemporary lamp standard with basket shade
              Sideboard. *On it:* pile of magazines, bottle of gin, copy of
                 New Statesman, bowl of flowers, decanter of whisky, jug of
                 water, 4 glasses, syphon of soda
                     In drawer: 5 table mats
                     On floor, leaning on L side of sideboard: tray
              Armchair. *On it:* Louise's handbag. *In it:* mirror, shooting bag
              Stool (R of armchair)
              3 upright chairs
              Upholstered bench
              Dining-table. *On it:* tablecloth, dish of butter with knife, dish
                 of marmalade with spoon, salt, pepper. *At upstage end of*
                 table: knife, fork, dessert spoon, side plate, ringed napkin,
                 pot of coffee, jug of milk. *At L of table:* copy of the *Daily*
                 Mail, cereal plate and dessert spoon, 2 knives, fork, side
                 plate, napkin out of ring, cup, saucer, tea spoon. *At down-*
                 stage end of table: side plate with knife, bread and butter,
                 cup with black coffee, saucer, tea spoon, napkin on chair,
                 napkin ring, ashtray, salver with sugar, cup, saucer and
                 tea spoon. *Down R side of table:* napkin in ring. *Up R side of*
                 table: napkin out of ring

              3 wall-brackets
              Light switch L of kitchen door
              Carpet on floor
              Window curtains and pelmet

              In schoolroom: table. *On it:* school textbooks, exercise-books,
                 2 pencils, list of history questions
              2 upright chairs
              Bookshelves. *On them:* books, gilt pot, blue and white mug,
                 teddy-bear, matches
              Built-in gas-fire
              Window curtains
              Door curtain
              Carpet on floor
              On wall R: ornamental clock
              Light bracket
              Light switch L of entrance

On landing: light bracket and switch
Runner on floor

In hall: small table. *On it:* telephone
Barometer
Clothes pegs. *On them:* Stanley's hat and mackintosh,
Louise's shawl, Pamela's hunting cap and riding
crop
Living-room window curtains open
French windows open
Kitchen door ajar
Hall door closed
Schoolroom window curtains open
Bedroom door in schoolroom closed
Schoolroom entrance curtain closed
Gas-fire off
Landing bedroom door closed
All light fittings off

Off stage: Plate of scrambled eggs (LOUISE)
Box of cartridges (STANLEY)
Plate of scrambled eggs (LOUISE)
Bunch of wild flowers (WALTER)
Music album (LOUISE)
Tray. *On it:* 5 clean knives, 5 clean forks (CLIVE)

Personal: CLIVE: lighter
STANLEY: pipe
WALTER: spectacles

SCENE 2

Strike: Everything from dining-table except ashtray
History list and papers from sofa
Tray from sideboard
Cartridge box from sideboard
Change flowers

Reset: Armchair down RC
Stool to L of armchair

Set: Tobacco jar on sideboard
Cigarette-box, matches and lighter to shelf under coffee-table
Copy of *Golf* on stool
Copy of *House and Garden* on sofa
Book of Essays on dining-table
Gramophone record on sideboard

Suitcase and scarf on floor R of sideboard
Cup of coffee on stool
Stanley's hat and coat on pegs in hall
On coffee-table: tray with pot of coffee, 2 cups, saucers and tea
spoons, bowl of sugar
Bowl of fruit on dining-table
All window curtains closed
Kitchen door closed
French windows closed
Hall door closed
Bedroom door in schoolroom closed
Schoolroom entrance curtain closed
Gas-fire off
Landing bedroom door closed
Light fittings on in living-room
Light fitting on landing on

Off stage: Brahms score (WALTER)
Tray. *On it:* clean forks and spoons (LOUISE)
Record catalogue (WALTER)
Tray. *On it:* silver pot of coffee, silver jug with milk, plate of
petit fours, bowl of sugar, coffee-cup, saucer and spoon,
ashtray, Louise's rings (LOUISE)

Personal: STANLEY: cigar
WALTER: matches, spectacles

ACT II

SCENE I

Strike: Dirty glasses
Coffee, tray, etc.
Essay book
Everything from dining-table

Reset: Coffee-table to L end of sofa
Stool under sideboard
Armchair C

Set: On table: cloth. *At upstage end:* fish knife and fork, dessert spoon,
side plate, napkin in ring. *At downstage end:* napkin in ring.
At L side: coffee-cup, saucer and spoon, napkin out of ring,
cigarette. *Up R:* napkin out of ring, cup of coffee, saucer,
spoon, copy of *Sunday Times.* Down R: fish knife and fork, dessert
spoon, side plate, napkin in ring, ashtray, salver with pot of

coffee, jug of milk, sugar basin, 2 coffee-cups, saucers and spoons.
At upstage R *corner:* 2 plates with remains of kipper and 2 fish
knives and forks; bowl of fruit
In schoolroom; on chair R *of table:* pile of sheets, towel, pillow-cases,
Pamela's jersey. *On table:* sandwich-tin
All windows closed
Window curtains open
Kitchen door ajar
Other doors closed
Gas-fire off
Light fittings off

Off stage: Plate of cereal (WALTER)
             Tea-towel (WALTER)
             Pot of coffee (LOUISE)
             Stanley's hunting coat (PAMELA)
             Egg whisk (LOUISE)
             Plate of scrambled eggs and 1 fork (CLIVE)
             Brahms score (WALTER)

SCENE 2

Strike: Everything from table except bowl of fruit and ashtray
          Dirty plates, coffee tray, etc., from sideboard
          Linen from schoolroom
          Newspaper

Reset: Armchair RC
         Stool R of armchair. *On it:* box of cigarettes, lighter
         Coffee-table R end of sofa

Set: On pegs in hall: Louise's stole
All windows closed
Window curtains closed
Doors closed
Gas fire on
Light fittings on in schoolroom and landing
Light fittings off in living-room

Off stage: Dressing-gown, nightdress, slippers (PAMELA)
             Tray. *On it:* plate of sandwiches, beaker of milk (LOUISE)

Personal: WALTER: spectacles, watch

LIGHTING PLOT

Property fittings required: contemporary standard lamp with basket shade, 3 modern wall-brackets, 2 shaded swan-neck wall-brackets

Interior. The same scene throughout comprising a living-room, landing, schoolroom and a hall behind a scrim R

THE MAIN ACTING AREAS are in the living-room, at a banquette R, at an armchair C and at a dining-table L. In the schoolroom, at a table C; on the landing, back C; and in the hall behind a scrim R of the living-room

THE APPARENT SOURCES OF LIGHT are in the living-room: in daytime, french windows L and at night, by wall-brackets R and L and a standard lamp up C. In the schoolroom: in daytime, a window R and a skylight, and at night, a wall-bracket R. On the landing, a wall bracket C

ACT I, SCENE 1. An autumn morning

To open: All fittings off
General effect of autumn sunshine
Gas-fire off
Flood outside kitchen door, on
Flood behind scrim, off
Schoolroom, hall and landing dimmed

Cue 1   LOUISE and CLIVE exit   (Page 9)
Dim sitting-room lighting
Bring up lighting in hall, schoolroom and landing

Cue 2   WALTER and PAMELA go out of the schoolroom   (Page 12)
Fade schoolroom to ½
Dim out landing and hall
Bring up lighting in sitting-room

Cue 3   PAMELA enters the living-room   (Page 15)
Dim out schoolroom lights

ACT I, SCENE 2. Night

To open: Fittings in living-room on
Fittings on landing on
Other fittings off
Gas-fire off
Night effect outside windows
Flood outside kitchen door, on
Flood behind scrim, off
Schoolroom, hall and landing dimmed

Cue 4   CLIVE: "Protect?"   (Page 26)
              Snap out kitchen flood

Cue 5   LOUISE switches out wall-brackets L   (Page 26)
              Snap out wall-brackets L
              Snap out covering lights

Cue 6   STANLEY switches out wall-bracket R   (Page 38)
              Snap out wall-bracket R
              Snap out all remaining lighting except for a spot in the
                 footlights, presumed to be a gas-fire

ACT II, SCENE 1.   Morning

To open: Lights as opening of Act I

Cue 7   PAMELA: ". . . squiggles and blobs."   (Page 43)
              Bring up lighting on stairs and hall

Cue 8   LOUISE: ". . . and get dressed."   (Page 46)
              Bring up lights on landing and schoolroom

Cue 9   PAMELA: ". . . of those mornings."   (Page 51)
              Fade schoolroom lights to ½

Cue 10   WALTER: ". . . in here, Mrs Harrington."   (Page 57)
              Fade schoolroom and landing lights

ACT II, SCENE 2.   Night

To open: Gas-fire on
              Night effect outside windows
              Flood outside kitchen door on
              Flood behind scrim off
              Fittings in schoolroom and landing on
              Fittings in living-room off

Cue 11   LOUISE switches on wall-bracket R   (Page 61)
              Snap in wall-bracket R
              Snap in covering lights

Cue 12   CLIVE switches off wall-bracket R   (Page 65)
              Snap out wall-bracket R
              Snap out all lights except for the fire spot in the footlights

Cue 13   WALTER enters from the schoolroom   (Page 68)
              Fade schoolroom lights to ½

Cue 14   WALTER enters the living-room   (Page 68)
              Build lights up a little around armchair area

Cue 15   STANLEY switches out schoolroom light   (Page 70)
              Snap out schoolroom bracket
              Snap out covering lights

Cue 16   STANLEY switches on living-room lights   (Page 70)
              Snap in wall-brackets
              Snap in covering lights

Cue 17   PAMELA switches on schoolroom light   (Page 78)
          Snap in schoolroom bracket
          Snap in covering lights

Cue 18   CLIVE: "Go on."   (Page 78)
          Slow fade of lights in living-room followed by fade of
          *   lights on landing*

EFFECTS PLOT

ACT I

SCENE 1

Cue 1   CLIVE: "Your bow."   (Page 16)
Piano music. "Gavotte in D Minor; Bach: Sixth English Suite"

Cue 2   CLIVE: ". . . 'perhaps' about her."   (Page 17)
Music stops

SCENE 2

Cue 3   CLIVE: ". . . from British Railways."   (Page 19)
Sound of piano practice

Cue 4   STANLEY: ". . . what they want."   (Page 21)
Piano music finishes with a bang

Cue 5   STANLEY: ". . . enough to eat."   (Page 21)
Gramophone record of "Brahms Third Symphony, No. 3 in F Major, 1st Movement"

Cue 6   WALTER exits to bedroom   (Page 22)
Gramophone ceases

Cue 7   CLIVE: "Oh, my dear fellow . . ."   (Page 33)
Front door slams

ACT II

SCENE 1

Cue 8   CLIVE: "Your Majesty."   (Page 49)
Gramophone record of "Brahms Third Symphony, No. 3 in F Major, 2nd Movement"

Cue 9   PAMELA falls   (Page 50)
Music stops abruptly

Cue 10   PAMELA: ". . . breaks its leg."   (Page 51)
Music recommences

Cue 11   LOUISE: "Now, come along."   (Page 51)
Gramophone needle sticks

Cue 12   PAMELA: "I'm just off."   (Page 52)
            Music ceases

SCENE 2

Cue 13   LOUISE: ". . . I cared for."   (Page 76)
            Gramophone record of "Mahler's Symphony, No. 4, in G
                Major, 3rd Movement"

Cue 14   CLIVE: "Maman!"   (Page 77)
            Gramophone needle sticks

Cue 15   STANLEY exits to Walter's room   (Page 77)
            Music ceases abruptly

NOTES

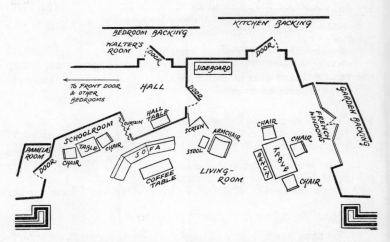

A simplified setting can be used, in which all the rooms are on the same level, with the schoolroom R. Most action which takes place on the landing now takes place in the hall. All references to stairs, "going up", etc., of course, to be cut, and in the very rare cases where this is necessary the appropriate phrase to be substituted in the text. The scene where PAMELA falls downstairs would now go as follows:

(PAMELA *enters the schoolroom from her bedroom, carrying her cap and crop and the hunting coat. She puts the cap on the back of her head, picks up her sandwich-tin from the table and goes into the hall, "conducting" the music with her crop and trailing the coat. She exits by the front door. The sound is heard of a crash off*)

PAMELA (*off*) Damn! Damn! Damn!

(*The music ceases abruptly.*
WALTER *rushes out of his room, startled by the crash*)

WALTER (*running to the front door*) What's the matter, Pamela? I help you.

(WALTER *exits by the front door*)

(*Off*) Are you hurt?
PAMELA (*off*) Of course not. Walter—put me down.

(WALTER *enters by the front door, carrying* PAMELA *in his arms. He goes into the schoolroom and deposits her on the chair* L *of the table. LOUISE *enters from the kitchen, carrying an egg whisk.* CLIVE *follows her on.* LOUISE *pauses a moment and hands the whisk to Clive*)

LOUISE. Here, take this. (*She crosses to the hall door*) Pamela! Pamela! What's the matter?

PAMELA (*irritated*) Anyone would think I was dying. (*She feels her head*) Ow!

WALTER. See? You bumped your head.

PAMELA (*witheringly*) When you fall down, you must bump something. It's usual.

WALTER. I look.

PAMELA. No.

(LOUISE *comes into the schoolroom.* CLIVE *follows to the hall door, listens a moment, then closes the door, crosses and exits to the kitchen*)

LOUISE (*moving between Pamela and Walter*) My darling, are you all right? What happened, Walter?

WALTER (*concerned*) She fell. I think you should look on her head.

LOUISE. Thank you, Walter. I'll see to it.

(WALTER *goes into the hall, collects Pamela's crop, cap, tin of sandwiches and coat, hands them to Louise, gives his half bow and exits to his room*)

PAMELA. Fuss, fuss, fuss.

(LOUISE *puts the crop, cap and tin on the table and the coat on the chair* R *of the table*)

LOUISE (*examining Pamela's head*) Let me see. Does it hurt?

PAMELA. No, it doesn't.

LOUISE. You say that as if you wanted it to. What on earth were you doing?

PAMELA (*exasperated*) Nothing. I just, etc.

On 21st September 1959 the play was entirely re-produced at the Comedy Theatre with a new cast and a new Director, Peter Wood. Mr. Wood found it useful to re-arrange the furniture on the set: the sofa and coffee table virtually exchanged places with the dining table and chairs (though of course the sofa was placed a little further down stage). The playing area for all the scenes centring around the sofa was thus enlarged.

MADE AND PRINTED IN GREAT BRITAIN BY WHITSTABLE
LITHO, STRAKER BROTHERS LTD. WHITSTABLE